CHESAPEAKE KALEIDOSCOPE

Chesapeake Kaleidoscope

Anne M. Hays
Harriet R. Hazleton

Illustrations by Mary J. Hazleton

TIDEWATER PUBLISHERS
Centreville   Maryland

Library of Congress Cataloging in Publication Data

Hays, Anne M   1933-
    Chesapeake Kaleidoscope.

    Bibliography: p.
    Includes index.
    1. Chesapeake Bay region. I. Hazleton, Harriet
R., 1913- joint author. II. Title.
    F187.C5H38   975.5'18   75-23447
    ISBN 0-87033-214-7

Cover photograph courtesy of Maryland Division of Tourist
Development, Department of Economic and Community
Development.

Manufactured in the United States of America
First edition, 1975; Second printing, 1982

CONTENTS

LIST OF ILLUSTRATIONS

ACKNOWLEDGMENTS

This book could not have been written without the support and constructive criticism offered by our families, to whom we are very grateful and dedicate this book.

Our thanks also go to the many people who helped us during our search for facts to interest and delight our readers.

Our special thanks for their willing help go to the personnel of the Virginia Institute of Marine Science, the Maryland Department of Natural Resources, the Virginia State Travel Service, the Maryland Division of Tourism, the United States Corps of Engineers, the Chesapeake Biological Laboratory, the Mariners Museum, and several libraries, including those of Calvert County, Kent County, Chestertown, Washington College, and the Maryland Hall of Records and Fairfax County's Virginia Room.

INTRODUCTION

Chesapeake Kaleidoscope is a book for people who want to know interesting, unusual, significant, and amusing facts about Chesapeake Bay.

The book will tell you things like: why Bay oysters sometimes turn pink or green; where to look for Blackbeard's buried treasure around the Bay; when and where to go to see a crab race; where a unique ferry ran that was half as long as the width of the river it crossed; and where there were Dutch-style windmills and tide mills which the colonists used to grind their grain.

Chesapeake Kaleidoscope offers you a cross section of history and humor, ecology and economics, geology and "gone fishin'."

Because the view is so broad, it cannot also be comprehensive, and many facts have necessarily been omitted. If we have left out some of your favorite ones, we would enjoy hearing from you about them, c/o Tidewater Publishers, P. O. Box 456, Centreville, Md. 21617.

Because times change, so may some of the items printed here. For example, by the time you read this, there may be a new oyster shucking champion, catches of crabs may have surpassed previous ones and new museums may have opened to commemorate some important facets of the past hitherto unrecognized.

We mention this so that you might be aware that such timely bits of information as operating hours for a particular attraction or a date for a local festival should be checked before setting out on an excursion with camera in hand and family in tow.

Our hope is that you will enjoy this book as it is intended—as an introduction to Chesapeake Bay and a companion to accompany you as you explore its byways by land or water.

I. THE BAY: PAST, PRESENT AND FUTURE

Physical Phenomena

Chesapeake Bay is 195 miles long and is either 37.5 miles or 22 miles across at its widest point, near the mouth of the Potomac River, depending on how you measure it.

At the widest point, the Bay is 9.75 feet higher in the center than on either side because of the earth's curvature.

The Bay is narrowest, only 4 miles across, at the William Preston Lane, Jr. Memorial Bridge, near Annapolis, a fact which might be disputed by motorists making the crossing during peak traffic periods.

The surface area of Chesapeake Bay is 4,316 square miles, or nearly one-tenth the combined size of the two bordering states, Maryland and Virginia.

For scientific and planning purposes, Chesapeake Bay includes the headwaters of the Susquehanna River in western New York, 400 miles away from what looks like the northern end of the Bay on a map, and extends south out into the Atlantic Ocean where the Bay's tides begin.

Chesapeake Bay is the drowned valley of the Susquehanna River which, ages ago, flowed directly into the Atlantic Ocean. The river valley became Chesapeake Bay either because the land suddenly sank, or because the level of the seas rose when the glaciers melted during the last Ice Age, about 15,000 to 18,000 years ago, or because of both. Scientists are not sure and do not agree on what happened, even though Chesapeake Bay, the largest estuary in the United States, is also said to be the most studied estuary in the world.

Chesapeake Bay fits the definition of both a bay and an estuary. An estuary is a place where fresh water from rivers mingles with salty tidal water from the ocean. A bay is a body of water partly surrounded by land.

The land surrounding Chesapeake Bay is sinking at about 1 foot or more per 100 years. No towns are immediately endangered, but it should be noted that because the slope of the coastal zone is quite flat, when the land sinks enough to be inundated, the shoreline may move inland many times the distance of the subsidence.

The land is sinking faster in the Virginia section of the Bay than in the Maryland section. At Smithfield, Va., the land is sinking at the rate of 18 inches per century. At Queenstown, the fastest sinking town in

1

Maryland, the land is sinking at the rate of 11.4 inches per century. Other Maryland towns, Annapolis and Havre de Grace, are sinking at about 9 inches per century. Solomons and Salisbury, Md., are sinking at about 10 inches per century. Cambridge, Md., is sinking at 8.4 inches per century.

———

Two of the scientists studying the formation of Chesapeake Bay have theorized why three Eastern Shore rivers, the Chester, the Miles, and the Choptank, all flow southwest but swing northwest before entering the Bay. With the use of high energy soundings, they discovered an older channel of the Susquehanna River, lying east of the present Bay

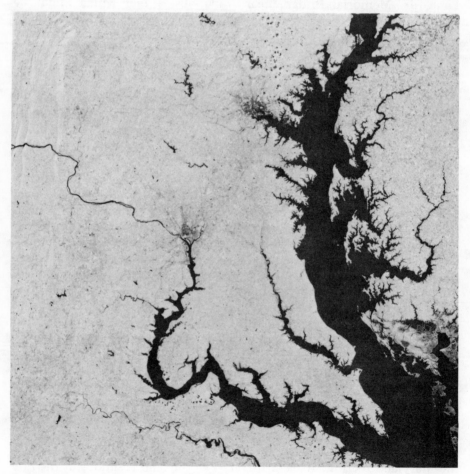

This satellite photograph of the upper Bay clearly shows the swing to the northwest which the Chester, the Miles, and the Choptank Rivers all take before entering the Bay. National Oceanic and Atmospheric Administration

channel and 50 to 100 feet below the present Bay bottom. The three rivers all flow into this old channel for a short distance before flowing into the present Bay channel.

Earthquakes have only occasionally occurred in the vicinity of Chesapeake Bay in recorded time, and all of these have been mild.

The earliest reported Bay area earthquake was centered in the Annapolis area on April 24, 1758.

St. Mary's City, in southern Maryland, and Round Bay, on the Severn River, have also been centers of mild earthquakes.

In 1855, several lighthouse keepers reported feeling the mild tremors of an earthquake. The keeper of the Hooper Strait Lighthouse reported feeling a shock which lasted about one and a half minutes, beginning at 9:51 p.m., Aug. 31, 1855.

Major earthquakes which have occurred elsewhere but which have been felt in the Bay area include one in Charleston, S.C., in August of 1886, which was equal to or greater than the 1906 earthquake in San Francisco.

The most recent earthquake to be felt in the Bay area was centered in Wilmington, Del., on Feb. 10, 1973.

Forty-eight rivers with 102 branches and tributaries flow into Chesapeake Bay and are navigable for 1,750 miles.

Twenty-four of these rivers are in Virginia and 24 are in Maryland. Maryland's share gives her more miles of river frontage than any of the other 49 states.

The largest and longest river flowing into Chesapeake Bay is the Susquehanna.

The Potomac is the second longest river flowing into the Bay.

The other seven of the nine major river streams flowing into the Bay are: the Choptank, the Nanticoke, the Pocomoke, the Patuxent, the Rappahannock, the York and the James, according to the United States Corps of Engineers.

The channel through the Bay is 161 miles long, and so straight the compass on a ship following it will vary only two points, or about 23 degrees. The channel has an authorized depth of 42 feet from the Capes to Baltimore.

At any moment the Bay contains about 18 trillion gallons of water. Approximately 45 billion gallons of surface water flow in and out of the Bay on an average day.

Chesapeake Bay water is notoriously murky, and the murk is caused primarily by large numbers of phytoplankton (microscopic plants) present in the water that interfere with the transmission of light.

———

The average depth of Chesapeake Bay is less than 28 feet. The deepest place in the Bay is near Bloody Point, where the water is 174 feet deep. This hole is one of several deep, stagnant pools formed millions of years ago when the Atlantic Coast sank. The water in these holes changes only once about every ten years, during unusually violent

Bloody Point Light

weather. Currents deflect silt from them so they do not fill in. Scientists speculate that horseshoe crabs live there, but fish probably do not.

———

The saltiness of Chesapeake Bay water varies considerably from north to south, from east to west, from top to bottom, and from summer to winter.

The Bay is saltier at the southern end of the Bay, where it flows into the Atlantic Ocean, than at its northern end. Thus the specific gravity of the water is 1.020 at Cape Henry as compared with 1.0020—1.0075 at Baltimore. As a result of this decrease in salinity and specific gravity, the water in Baltimore is less buoyant than the water at Cape Henry. A large freighter will float in 1 foot less water at Cape Henry than in Baltimore because of this decrease in the water's specific gravity.

Water is saltier on the Eastern Shore of Chesapeake Bay than on the Western Shore, partly because of the earth's rotation, and partly because of the tremendous freshwater flow from the Bay's major tributaries on the Western Shore.

Of the total area drained by the Bay, 64,170 square miles, the Susquehanna River, which is the largest river on the east coast of the United States, drains 42 percent, the Potomac River drains 22 percent, and the Rappahannock-York-James Rivers system drains 24 percent. Thus these Western Shore rivers collect water from 88 percent of the total area which drains into the Bay.

Because salty water is heavier than fresh water, Chesapeake Bay water is saltier at the bottom than at the top. The salty water coming into the Bay from the ocean has a net movement on the bottom up the Bay. The fresher water flowing in from the rivers tends to stay on top and has a net movement down the Bay.

When rainfall swells the Bay's main tributaries, more fresh water flows into the Bay than during dry seasons, diluting and decreasing the Bay's salinity.

This change in Bay salinity sets up a nontidal circulation between the Bay and its smaller tributaries which have small freshwater inflow. When Bay salinity is high, Bay water flows along the bottom into tributaries. This action forces bottom water from the tributaries back into the Bay as a non-tidal current.

Normally the Bay water is saltiest during late summer and fall. It is less salty in winter and spring. _____

Tidal currents help to prevent stagnation by their flushing action. The average maximum tidal current on the Bay ranges from 0.5 knots to over 2 knots in different parts of the Bay. Ebb tide runs about 6.5 hours, and flood tide runs about 5.9 hours.

The ebb current is normally stronger than the flood current. For example, the flood current is about 1.0 knots at the entrance to Chesapeake Bay, and the ebb current is about 1.5 knots at the same place. The flood current is about 0.6 knots at the Craighill Channel Entrance en route to Baltimore, and the ebb current there is 0.7 knots.

A vessel entering Chesapeake Bay at a speed of 12 knots can pass Cape Henry two or three hours before high tide at that point and carry a favorable current all the way to Baltimore. The same ship could leave Baltimore at the same speed at high tide and carry a favorable current almost two-thirds of the way to Cape Henry.

Chesapeake Bay weather history contains more folklore than fact. Reliable information concerning the highest wind velocity, high and low temperatures, rainfall records, occurrence of waterspouts, etc., is not available because no stations to record these phenomena exist out on the Bay. Even manned lighthouses, such as the one at Thomas Point, have never had instruments to record the weather accurately.

During the summer of 1974, an effort was made to correlate existing surface weather conditions with the information received from a weather satellite providing a continuous, 24-hour view of the weather over the Bay. To do this, the National Oceanic and Atmospheric Administration enlisted the aid of the Coast Guard, marinas, state parks, military installations, and commercial and private boats to regularly report current weather conditions, temperature, wind direction, and speed.

For the two months this program was pursued, this information was compiled into an hourly updated report of the current weather and a short term (0 to 6 hours) forecast. This was broadcast over channel KEC 83 (162.40MHz), the continuous weather channel.

The most common time for thunderstorms on Chesapeake Bay is 4 p.m. during June, July and August. Each of these months has an average of seven storms, lasting about 30 minutes each. An anvil-shaped cloud building in the southwest to northwest issues a warning.

The first recorded Chesapeake Bay sailor's storm story came from Capt. John Smith, who commented on nearly every aspect of Bay life observed during his 1608 explorations.

"Our mast and sail blew overboard and such mighty waves overraked us in that small barge that with great danger we kept her from sinking by freeing out the water."

Violent Bay storms are sometimes described as Tom Smith weather. Tom Smith was the captain of William Claiborne's *Long Tayle*, the first sailing boat built on the Chesapeake. If you can see the *Long Tayle* on the horizon, its white sails showing against the black clouds, it's Tom Smith weather, and you should seek the nearest shelter.

Severe storms were recorded by the colonists on Chesapeake Bay in 1667, 1688, 1749, 1761, and 1769. A flood which accompanied a storm in 1771 caused an estimated two million pounds sterling damage.

On Aug. 22, 1933, a hurricane struck the Bay. High tides and winds caused great damage to shore communities and boats. Not forewarned of the storm as they would be today, two Old Bay Line steamers, *The State of Maryland* and *The City of Norfolk*, had left Baltimore together. When the storm hit, *The City of Norfolk* went aground near Watts Island in Pocomoke Sound trying to get safely in the lee of the

Eastern Shore. Her passengers were rescued. *The State of Maryland* was able to continue down the Bay and make port in Norfolk. When they arrived, they found the city flooded. Most of the passengers stayed aboard the ship a few days until the water subsided.

The most recent hurricane to hit Chesapeake Bay was Agnes, during the week of June 14, 1972. The National Oceanic and Atmospheric Administration called the storm and its aftermath one of the worst natural disasters in United States history. Maryland and Virginia were among the states hardest hit, with Maryland and the District of Columbia combined recording 21 deaths and storm damage of $110,000,000, and Virginia recording 13 deaths and storm damage of $220,000,000.

The Bay itself suffered from the large quantities of fresh rainwater, which lowered the salinity of the Bay water and devastated the shellfish industry.

As a natural compensation, the reduced salinity also destroyed shellfish parasites, particularly MSX and oyster drills, and Virginia Institute of Marine Science scientists expected increased survival of wild spatfalls and healthier oysters for at least a few years as a result.

Agnes' high tides and winds also took a heavy toll of shorelines and Bayside property.

———

Winters on the Bay seem milder in recent years than in former ones. Pictures of sleighs driving down the streets of Chestertown, Md., and boats marooned in the ice look unreal, yet many severe snowstorms and instances of icing have been recorded.

Father Andrew White, who arrived in Maryland when the first colonists came on the *Ark* and the *Dove*, was the first to record the Potomac River being frozen over, in 1642.

During the winter of 1732-33, an Annapolis man recorded he could not sail for London until March because of the ice.

During the winter of 1746-47, a historian reported that Bay creeks and rivers were frozen solidly for seven weeks.

During the winter of 1780-81, ice on the Bay was 6 inches thick from the Elk River to the mouth of the Potomac River. People traveled between Annapolis and Rock Hall, and Poplar, Kent, and Tilghman Islands by cart or carriage across the ice instead of by boat for several weeks.

In 1814, loaded wagons could safely cross the Potomac River on the ice.

Trains were usually ferried across in those days, but, between Jan. 15 and Feb. 24, 1852, 1,378 railroad cars ran across the Susquehanna River from Havre de Grace on track laid over the ice.

If you wanted to, reports say you could walk from Washington, D.C., to Norfolk, Va., on the iced-over Bay during the winter of 1856-57.

The great blizzard of March 1888 caused considerable damage. On the Eastern Shore several vessels sank, and others were driven ashore. Twenty-five lives were lost.

Temperatures dropped to —8° F. in Chestertown, Md., during the great blizzard of February 1889. When temperatures rose, the snow turned to rain, flooding cellars and streams.

In 1914, two men in a boat frozen in Canoe Neck Creek on the Potomac River were picked up by a Navy patrol boat. Officials discovered then that they were German spies who were mapping the Bay and its tributaries.

Another blizzard struck the Bay in January 1922. Railroads, the principal means of transportation and communication for many towns then, could not run for several days.

Chesapeake Bay has not iced over completely since 1936, when it was frozen for 80 miles, almost as far south as the Patuxent River. Bay tributaries as far south as the James River were frozen, and fields of drift ice floated between the Virginia Capes.

———

Waterspouts are occasionally seen on the Chesapeake. They are caused by the low pressure area in the center of a tornado passing over a body of water. Water may be sucked up into the funnel as high as 200 feet.

A waterspout was recorded on Chesapeake Bay in November, 1970. In mid-Bay, the 112-foot cruise ship, the *Mount Hope*, out of Warren, R.I., was threatened by a series of small waterspouts. The captain immediately headed for Solomons, the nearest deepwater port. Those twisting, dark clouds rising ominously into the air caused the passengers to finish their cruise by bus.

The Changing Bay Environment

Capt. John Smith may have been recording what we would call a fish kill when he wrote in the early 1600's: "That abundance of fish, lying so thicke with their heads above the water as for want of nets . . . we attempted to catch them with a frying pan. . . ."

Because of the increased temperatures and light of summer, the Bay water sometimes becomes supersaturated with gases, producing a gas embolism disease in fish which causes them to swim close to the surface as Smith described. Today we also have fish kills due to a high concentration of pesticides in the water, accidental spillage of industrial wastes, and faulty sewage systems.

In August of 1973, the large fish kill which occurred in the James River, near the mouth of the Warwick River, was found to be the result of excessive chlorination at the Hampton Roads Sanitation District's

James River sewage treatment plant. After rectifying this problem, the Marine Resources Commission then began to wonder what effect the chlorine level had on oyster larvae. The problem was studied by several cooperating agencies, and it was decided to reduce the normal chlorine level by half during the oyster spawning season. A normal oyster set was achieved without the necessity of condemning any adjacent waters.

Fish kills can also be caused by the mahogany tide which occurs occasionally in the Bay during hot weather. The mahogany tide is caused by the presence of large numbers of small organisms which turn the water brown or mahogany-colored, and use up so much of the oxygen supply that there is not enough left for the fish.

––––––

The present population of more than 15 million people dwelling in the area draining into Chesapeake Bay is projected to more than double in numbers, perhaps as soon as the turn of the century. More and better treatment of sewage will be required before it is dumped into the Bay if the present level of water pollution is not to be exceeded.

Ships in transit also add to the Bay's pollution. In June of 1970, it was estimated that the raw sewage discharged into the Bay from ships in transit is equivalent at all times to that which can be discharged by a community of 25,000 people.

Petroleum, coming from accidental spills, industrial runoff, and discharge from the bilge tanks of ships, is one of the chief threats to the ecology of the Bay. Two University of Maryland scientists have identified some marine microorganisms which are capable of degrading petroleum. They are studying the possibility of seeding spills with these specific fungi, yeasts, and bacteria which work together to convert petroleum into ecologically harmless elements.

Oil spills are a form of pollution which particularly affects the waterfowl population. In 1970, the Coast Guard estimated over one million gallons of oil were spilled into Chesapeake Bay. According to the Fish and Wildlife Service Report, oil spills have killed as many as 5,000 waterfowl at a time in the Baltimore area.

Livestock raised on land bordering Bay tributaries has been known to pollute the water through bacterial contamination of the runoff to such an extent that shellfish beds downstream have been closed.

Maryland was one of the first states to ban the use of DDT (in 1970) when it was suspected of contaminating the Bay through runoff from agricultural land and entering the food chain when ingested by simple organisms.

When Capt. John Smith described an Indian mining operation he observed on one of his voyages of exploration in the early 1600's as, "wherein they digged a great hole with shells and hatchets, and hard by it runneth a fayre brooke of christol-like water, where they wash away

This remarkably accurate map of Chesapeake Bay was drawn by Captain John Smith, who explored the Bay in 1612. U.S. Library of Congress

10

the drosse and keepe the remained, which they put in little baggs and sell it over the country to paint their bodyes, faces or idols," he was really talking about a commercial strip-mining venture, the effluent of which was an early man-induced pollutant of the Bay.

Sediment is one of the most dangerous pollutants threatening Bay waters.

Sediment, which is a product of erosion, is soil or other surficial (surface plus superficial) material transported or deposited by the action of wind, water, ice, or gravity.

Seventy to 80 percent of the year's sediment load is carried to Chesapeake Bay in February and March because of the heavy rainfalls which usually occur during those months.

Figures from the Maryland Department of Natural Resources tell us that even naturally forested land can lose as much as 100 tons of sediment per square mile through erosion per year. That same land, cleared for farming, will lose more. And the same land, cleared for a typical urban construction project, can lose as much as 200 tons of sediment per acre per year, or 128,000 tons of sediment per square mile per year.

As sediment drops out of the water at the mouths of rivers, it decreases the water depth there and causes fresh water to flow farther into the Bay, lowering the salinity there, which can kill oysters. Oysters at the mouths of rivers have also been smothered in severe cases of sedimentation.

To maintain the depth of Baltimore Harbor, 111,000,000 cubic yards of sediment have been removed from it at a cost of about $17,000,000 during the past one hundred years.

Dredging to maintain a channel has been going on continuously on the Potomac since 1804. The annual cost of this dredging is now around $150,000.

The results of sedimentation can be seen all around the Bay where towns which were once ports are landlocked or can claim only a trickle remaining in what were once navigable waters.

The small town of Dumfries on the Potomac River was a booming deepwater tobacco port in colonial days, rivaling New York City. When most of the men left before spring planting to join the Revolutionary War army, soil which washed off the cleared, unplanted fields filled up the creek. After the war, Quantico Creek was no longer navigable as far as Dumfries, and the town could no longer serve as a port.

By 1700, the virgin timber had been cut, and the town of Port Tobacco, on a Potomac River tributary, was surrounded by large plantations. From 1700 to 1775, it was one of the busiest seaports in America, on a par with Georgetown, Alexandria, and Annapolis. The

The water has become rather shallow in St. Michaels Harbor through the years. These unsuspecting yachts were left careened when the tide went out. Anne M. Hays

river gradually filled with sediment. In 1775, a visitor remarked that "the Port Tobacco Creek carries only small craft now." The town declined. It bustled once more when a new courthouse was built between 1819 and 1821, but faded when the railroad bypassed it, and La Plata became the county seat.

Joppatown, on the Gunpowder River, was the Baltimore County seat from 1712 to 1768. It was then a major tobacco exporting point and had a racetrack and an active social calendar. Timber cutting along the river allowed large quantities of soil to run off the land and fill in the harbor. The head of navigation moved downstream 2.5 miles. The town gradually disappeared.

So that our modern ports do not share the fate of Dumfries, Port Tobacco, and Joppatown, waterways must be dredged. Today there are more than one hundred federally-constructed navigation projects on the Bay and its tributaries which must be maintained. The problem of spoil disposal is a major deterrent to maintenance dredging.

In 1974, the Wicomico River channel leading to Salisbury had shoaled until barges were no longer able to carry a full load when navigating its waters.

Capt. Linwood T. Sadler, a barge captain, was charged with negligence by the Coast Guard after he brought a loaded petroleum barge up the river on a high tide, and it settled and ruptured, spilling about 25 gallons of oil when the tide went out before the barge was unloaded.

Commerce on the Wicomico River had doubled in the ten years prior to 1974 to a total of more than one million tons that year. Petroleum, fertilizer, grain, lumber, and other construction materials are the major products transported on the river. Money and lack of a spoil disposal site are the two major hurdles to dredging by the U.S. Corps of Engineers.

Sedimentation may occasionally work to your advantage. For example, during the War of 1812, the British intended to attack Easton, Md. The British tried to sail their warships up the Tred Avon River, but several of them went aground. They finally gave up the attempt, and Easton was saved by the river's shoals.

A single storm in 1680 caused sand and sediment to pile up and form Willoughby Spit at the mouth of the James River. Madame Thomas Willoughby claimed the newly formed land for her own, and thus it became known as Willoughby's Spit.

————

The tidal shoreline of Chesapeake Bay is about 4,600 miles. Of this number, about 3,400 miles of tidal shoreline are in Maryland and about 1,200 miles of tidal shoreline are in Virginia.

According to a study conducted by the U.S. Corps of Engineers, the Bay swallows about 326 acres of land from the shore each year and only gives back about 52 acres. Through this process of taking and giving, whole islands have been known to move, divide, or disappear.

Between 1845 and 1952, it is estimated that 6,000 acres of land were lost from Maryland's 230 miles of primary shoreline alone.

Traditionally landowners have tried to keep the Bay at bay by building bulkheads or jetties. Building a marsh to protect a shoreline is an ecologically oriented idea that is being used experimentally.

Environmental Concern, Inc., created a man-made marsh in 1972 on a one-acre lot on Hambleton Island, near St. Michaels, where the grass had disappeared and the sand was eroding. Swamp grasses were planted and protected until they had rooted sufficiently to withstand the action of the water. The shoreline has been stabilized, and the experiment is considered a success. As a result, several similar projects have been undertaken.

Sharp's Island Hotel

Erosion of parts of Tilghman Island seems to have been checked now by planting smooth cordgrass in rows along the shore.

Smith and Tangier Islands are known to have been joined at one time by a sandbar. Some people can still remember when Taylors and James Islands were connected. But between 1848 and 1910, James Island lost 385 acres, or about one-half its total area, and became separated from Taylors Island. Since that time, more than 150 additional acres have eroded into the Bay from James Island.

Hog Island, Va., had a population of 250 people before erosion took so much land that the people left.

Holland Island, in Holland Strait, had a population of about 300 and could boast of a church, a schoolhouse, and several stores. Around 1900, pieces of the island began to drop off into the Bay. About 1920, most of the families tore down their houses, loaded what they could salvage onto boats, and moved to the mainland because the water was licking so close to their doorsteps some housewives could throw the dishwater out of the kitchen window, directly into the Bay.

Sharps Island, now just a shallow spot marked by a lighthouse at the mouth of the Choptank River, was probably connected to Tilghman Island when the first European explorers came to the Bay. A colonial Maryland governor is said to have ridden his horse between the two islands. In 1850, the island, though separate from Tilghman Island, still had an area of about 600 acres, and several families lived and farmed there. In 1900, a hotel was built to accommodate summer visitors. By 1914, only about 100 acres of land were left, and in 1944, the federal government took over the remains—6 acres of marsh. This has since eroded away to below the water level.

St. Clement's Island, in the Potomac River, where the first Maryland colonists came ashore in 1634, was then probably ten times its present size of 40 acres. Now the shoreline has been stabilized, but the erosion control measures cost the state of Maryland $428,000.

Agencies and Organizations Concerned with the Bay

Anyone interested in learning about any aspect of Chesapeake Bay gradually discovers that his interest is shared by a startling number of federal, state, and local agencies, committees, foundations, and institutions.

For example, as many as 50 institutions and federal and state agencies are involved in data collection and analysis of the water quality of Chesapeake Bay and its tidal tributaries.

No single agency in either of the two bordering states, Maryland and Virginia, has final jurisdiction over that part of the Bay within its state boundaries.

———

Johns Hopkins' Chesapeake Bay Institute, the Virginia Institute of Marine Science, the University of Maryland's Chesapeake Biological Laboratory, and the Smithsonian Institution's Chesapeake Bay Center for Environmental Studies formed the Chesapeake Research Consortium as a nonprofit agency in January, 1972, to integrate and coordinate their research programs to avoid duplication and to provide better communication between the agencies.

The **Chesapeake Bay Institute** was established in 1948. Its primary area of study has been physical and chemical research in the Bay. Recently it has been conducting a study of plankton ecology combined with a chemical sampling program in the Upper Bay.

The **Virginia Institute of Marine Science** is a state-supported laboratory and a state regulatory agency which provides advice to the Virginia state government. Its work is multidisciplinary, including physical, chemical, and biological programs. It recently conducted a water quality study of the James River and has developed mathematical models of many of Virginia's tidal streams.

The **Chesapeake Bay Center for Environmental Studies,** set up in 1966 on the Rhode River, has been studying that watershed and contiguous wetlands. Their facilities are available to schoolteachers and students for study of human and natural ecology. The Center also operates a speakers bureau, drawing upon their staff to lecture to interested groups.

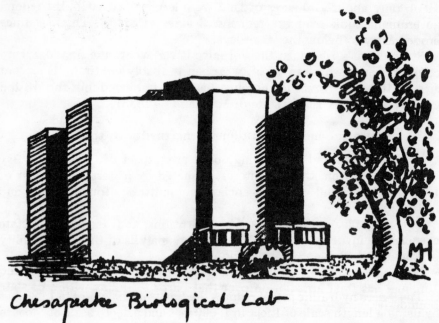

Chesapeake Biological Lab

The **Chesapeake Biological Laboratory (CBL),** established in 1925 in Solomons, is the oldest permanent state-supported marine biological laboratory in continuous use on the East Coast. CBL programs deal with ecosystem behavior, fisheries science and biology and environmental chemistry, biochemistry and toxicology.

The **Truitt Controlled Environment Laboratory** at the Chesapeake Biological Laboratory is a recent unique addition to marine laboratories along the East Coast. Dedicated in October 1974, the laboratory is named for Dr. Reginald V. Truitt who pioneered in researching Maryland's estuarine resources and founded the Chesapeake Biological Laboratory.

The laboratory has a dual seawater delivery system with a heat exchange system that can control temperatures over a range of 5° to 30° C. The design was planned to meet the needs of marine scientists for control and measurement of water temperature and salinity during experiments.

A brief description of some other agencies and organizations concerned with Chesapeake Bay which are likely to be of interest to individuals follows in alphabetical order.

The Center for Environmental and Estuarine Studies, at Horns Point on the Choptank River near Cambridge, was formed in 1973. The Center includes the Seafood Processing Laboratory at Crisfield, which is conducting research on the seafood of the Bay; the Chesapeake Biological Laboratory at Solomons, which is making estuarine studies; and the Environmental Laboratory at Horns Point, which is studying marsh ecology and shellfish aquaculture; as well as other agencies in the state of Maryland not involved with Chesapeake Bay affairs.

The two major goals of the Center are to conduct research into the causes and effects of environmental change and to provide pertinent information to the makers of the environmental policies.

The Chesapeake Bay Foundation is a nonprofit organization founded in 1966 to involve citizens in the care of the natural resources of Chesapeake Bay. The foundation does this by: emphasizing environmental education that exposes students to the Bay; representing the Bay community as unofficial ombudsman; developing waterfowl research; and encouraging private land philanthropy. The foundation has chapters in both Virginia and Maryland.

A tool for studying the physical reactions of the Bay to various natural and man-induced variations is the **Chesapeake Bay Model,** constructed at Matapeake by the U.S. Corps of Engineers.

The 9-acre hydraulic model reduces the Bay from 195 miles to 1,080 feet by using a length scale of 1 foot to 1, 000 feet and a depth scale of 1 foot to 100 feet.

The model has been used by the federal government and the states of Maryland, Virginia, and Pennsylvania to help define and provide a water/land management program for the Chesapeake Basin.

A hydraulic model of the James River is already in existence at the Waterways Experiment Station in Vicksburg, Miss. It was built to study such problems as how deepening the river channel from Hampton Roads to Richmond would affect the oyster industry. The Virginia

Hydraulic model of the James River constructed by the U.S. Corps of Engineers and located in Vicksburg, Miss. U.S. Corps of Engineers

Institute of Marine Science is a joint operator of this model with the Corps of Engineers.

Environmental Concern, Inc., is a nonprofit corporation founded in 1972, with the mission of maintaining or enhancing environmental quality through active programs of applied and basic research.

Specifically, they have been working to control erosion with man-made marshes. Their first project was at Hambleton Island, near St. Michaels. Another is on the Susquehanna Flats.

Planting beach cover

The National Marine Fisheries Laboratory at Oxford studies parasites and diseases of marine fish and shellfish. As a federal agency, their work includes, but is not confined to, local Bay problems. Brief tours are available by prior arrangement and an open house is held annually in October.

Save Our Streams (SOS) is sponsored by the Izaak Walton League of America, and has the goal of benefiting the fish population by cleaning up small streams. Since the pollution from the small streams finds its way into larger streams and eventually into the Bay, cleaning up these small streams will have a far-reaching effect.

Following is a list of addresses of the agencies and organizations previously described, as well as additional ones which might be useful to an individual investigating some particular aspect of Chesapeake Bay.

Federal Agencies

U.S. Army Engineer, Baltimore District
Corps of Engineers
P. O. Box 1715
Baltimore, MD 21203
(301) 962-2020

Department of the Army
Norfolk District, Corps of Engineers
803 Front Street
Norfolk, VA 23510
(804) 625-8201

National Marine Fisheries Service
Biological Laboratory
Oxford, MD 21654
(301) 226-5193

United States Coast Guard
5th Coast Guard District
Federal Building
431 Crawford Street
Portsmouth, VA 23705

State, City and Area Tourism Information

Tourist Development Office
Maryland Department of Economic and
    Community Development
1748 Forest Dr.
Annapolis, MD 21401
(301) 269-2686

Virginia State Travel Service
911 East Broad Street
Richmond, VA 23219

Peninsula Chamber of Commerce (Newport
    News and Hampton)
1800 Mercury Blvd, Coliseum Mall A-12
Hampton, VA 23666

Eastern Shore Chamber of Commerce
Accomac, VA 23301

Annapolis Chamber of Commerce
171 Conduit Street
Annapolis, MD 21401
(301) 268-7676

Baltimore Office of Tourism and Promotion
110 W. Baltimore St.
Baltimore, MD 21201
(301) 752-8632

Private and State Organizations and Agencies Concerned with Chesapeake Bay

The Center for Environmental and
    Estuarine Studies
P. O. Box 775, Horn Pt. Rd.
Cambridge, MD 21613
(301) 228-8200

Chesapeake Bay Bridge and Tunnel District
P. O. Box 111
Cape Charles, VA 23310

Chesapeake Bay Center for Environmental
    Studies
P. O. Box 28
Edgewater, MD 21037
(301) 798-4424

Chesapeake Bay Foundation
162 Prince George Street
Annapolis, MD 21401
(301) 268-8816

Chesapeake Bay Institute
4800 Atwell Rd.
Shady Side, MD 29764
(301) 867-7550

Chesapeake Biological Laboratory
Box 38
Solomons, MD 20688

Environmental Concern, Inc.
P.O. Box P
St. Michaels, MD 21663
(301) 745-9620

The Maryland Historical Trust
21 State Circle
Annapolis, MD 21401
(301) 269-2213

Virginia Division of Mineral Resources
Natural Resources Bldg.
McCormich Road
Charlottesville, VA 22903

Virginia Institute of Marine Science
Gloucester Point
Virginia, 23602
(804) 642-2111

Virginia Marine Resources Commission
2401 West Avenue
Newport News, VA 23607
(804) 245-2811

Virginia State Water Control Board
2109 N. Hamilton St.
Richmond, VA 23230
(804) 257-0056

Maryland Department of Natural Resources
Tawes State Office Building
Annapolis, MD 21401
(301) 269-2230

Save Our Streams (SOS)
Izaak Walton League of America
1800 N. Kent St.
Arlington, VA 22201
(703) 528-1818

Virginia Port Authority
234 Monticello Ave.
Suite 1600, Maritime Tower
Norfolk, VA 23510
(804) 622-1671

Maryland Port Administration
The World Trade Center
Baltimore, MD 21202
(301) 383-3010

Virginia Historical Society
Boulevard and Kensington Ave.
P.O. Box 7311
Richmond, VA 23221

II. EXPLORING CHESAPEAKE BAY

The First Europeans and Those Who Followed

The first European to see Chesapeake Bay may have been the Irishman, St. Brendan, who, according to legend, traveled across the ocean in the sixth century in a hide-covered boat called a coracle.

A Viking, Thorfinn Karlsefni, may have discovered the Bay when he explored the East Coast of North America in the eleventh century, but no real evidence exists that he did.

John Cabot, exploring for King Henry VII of England, may have sailed into Chesapeake Bay in 1498.

In 1524, Giovanni Verrazano anchored his ship in Chincoteague Bay and walked overland eight miles to the headwaters of the Pocomoke River. He got close, but he probably did not see Chesapeake Bay itself.

In 1526, Spaniards led by Ayallon established a settlement called San Miguel de Gualdape. The settlement, troubled by internal strife and disease, was soon abandoned. It stood on or near the site where the English later established Jamestown.

Spanish expeditions returned to Chesapeake Bay, which they called St. Mary's Bay, in 1570, 1571, 1573, and 1588. Spanish Jesuit priests from the 1570 expedition settled on the York River, but all were killed by Indians after only five months.

In 1585, Capt. Lane, from Raleigh's colony in Carolina, rediscovered Chesapeake Bay for the English.

The first white men to fully explore the Bay may have been Spaniards led by Vincente Gonzales. Gonzales was sent by Mendenez de Aviles, governor of the Spanish colony in Florida, to investigate possible English settlements. Gonzales circumnavigated the Bay and described what he saw, but left no charts. The expedition is variously dated as 1566 and 1588.

Bartholomew Gilbert, a nephew of Sir Walter Raleigh, was killed by Indians while searching for fresh water on the Virginia Eastern Shore on July 29, 1603. He sailed into Chesapeake Bay to look for survivors of the lost Roanoke Colony.

———

The Cape Henry Memorial, a cross marking the place where the Jamestown colonists first set foot in America, is near Virginia Beach, a few hundred yards from the Cape Henry Lighthouse.

After touching shore there, the colonists sailed 32 miles up the James River where they founded the first permanent English settlement in North America on May 13, 1607.

The settlement, called Jamestown, was located on a marshy penin-sula, now an island. The first buildings were a triangular blockhouse and several huts. Burned in 1608, they were rebuilt and added to by 1609. The colonists nearly starved during the winter of 1609-10, and the colony would have been abandoned except for the timely arrival in June 1610 of Lord De la Warr (Delaware) with more colonists and supplies.

Cape Henry Cross

Jamestown eventually was deserted after burning several times and after the state capital was moved to Williamsburg in 1699.

The first colonists sent to Virginia by the London Company held their property in common. In 1610, Sir Thomas Dale, then governor of Virginia, divided this communal land among the individual colonists. He thus established the right of individual ownership of property in the New World.

By 1675, all the land available on Virginia's Eastern Shore had been assigned.

Since at that time Virginia's boundaries were considered to be: on the North, the Potomac River; on the South, the settlement of North Carolina; on the East, the Atlantic Ocean, called the Virginia Sea; and on the West, the "California Sea, whenever the settlements shall be extended so far, or now by the River Mississippi," there was still plenty of land available on the Western Shore.

The population of Virginia in 1650 was estimated to be 20,000; in 1670, 40,000; by 1700, it was 70,000; in 1730, 114,000. In 1755, a century after the first population estimate, 294,000 or nearly 15 times as many people inhabited the area.

In Maryland, Lord Baltimore gave each colonist who paid his own way over from England 100 acres of land, plus 100 acres for each adult he transported up to the number of four, and 50 acres for each child under 16 years. If five or more adults came, 2,000 acres were awarded, and if 20 or more were brought, larger land grants were offered. But, like many real estate ventures, so many people came that Lord Baltimore cut the grants in half after 1641 and stopped giving them entirely after 1689.

In 1660, the population of Maryland was estimated to be 8,000 settlers; in 1700, 32,000. By 1715, the number had reached 50,200. In 1775, the population had increased twenty-five-fold, to a total of 200,000 persons.

How They Named What They Found

The unusual names of some estates, towns, islands, points, rivers and creeks around the Bay are tantalizing. Who gave them these names? And why?

Sometimes statements conflict, each claiming to be historically correct. Many of them have Indian names or were named for an early settler who owned the land. Others were named in honor of a prominent citizen, a saint, or even an enemy. Some took their name from an event at that location, a feature of the land, a ship that went aground, or even a ferryboat or steamer that docked there.

Most authorities agree that the name Chesapeake is of Indian origin, but they disagree about the exact word derivation or what it meant. Three explanations of how the Bay came to be known as Chesapeake are: 1) from Tschischiwapeki—meaning highly salted body of standing water, a pond or bay, also "Great Waters"; 2) from Chesapiooc—meaning country on a great river; 3) from Chesapeack—meaning "Mother of Waters."

The Western Shore Indians called the Eastern Shore Accomack, meaning "on the other side of the water place."

Yeocomico, a tributary flowing into the often rough mouth of the Potomac River, meant "tossed to and fro by the waters" to the Indians.

The first Lord Baltimore, George Calvert, wanted to name his land grant in the New World Crescentia. But Charles I, who made the grant, suggested it be named after his wife, Queen Henrietta Maria. So it was called Terra Mariae, or Maryland.

Virginia was named by Queen Elizabeth in 1584 in her own honor as the Virgin Queen.

Col. Henry Coursey came to Maryland in 1653 and, in return for his support of Lord Baltimore in the Battle of Horn's Point, he was offered all the land he could cover on a map with his thumb. Henry Coursey had the good judgment to apply his thumb to about 1,600 acres on the bank of the Chester River. He gratefully named his large estate "My Lord's Gift."

Bloody Point is a name which has inspired at least two gory explanations. One is that a notorious French pirate was hanged at this Kent Island spot. Another claimed that Indians were massacred there by colonists who lured them to the scene by promising a parley.

For old times' sake, so they say, John Smith named Tangier Island after the Tangier pirates he had been unfriendly with in years past. Other sources tell that Smith named the island Russell's Island after Dr. Russell who accompanied him on his voyage of exploration.

Tradition tells that the first settler bought Tangier Island from the Indians for two greatcoats, but the Indians disliked the bargain and reclaimed the island.

The first permanent settlement by white men on the island was in 1666 when five men and their families from Cornwall, England, settled there.

By 1970, about 900 people lived on the island.

When Capt. Nathaniel Utie came from Virginia with a license to trade with the Indians in the Upper Bay in the seventeenth century, he came with a lot of hope for the success of his venture. And so he renamed the island where he settled, calling it Spesutie Island, a combination of the Latin spes, meaning hope, and his own name, Utie.

Rock Hall probably took its name from an estate in the area which was built partly of stone. The town was founded in 1707, and was a way-stop for travelers between Philadelphia and Williamsburg in Colonial days. From Rock Hall, George Washington made the 25-mile trip by boat to Annapolis at least eight times. Once he was stranded overnight on the boat when it went aground in a storm on the Horn Point shoal just off Annapolis harbor.

Thomas Jefferson also crossed from Annapolis to Rock Hall by ferry in 1766, when he was 23 years old. The story goes that he was on his way to Philadelphia for a smallpox inoculation.

The town of Gratitude was originally called Deep Landing, a name with promise of a safe, shoal-free berth. Perhaps that is what enticed Philadelphia-bound steamboats to stop there. When the steamboat did begin to put in regularly, the name of the town was changed to Gratitude—the name of the steamboat.

Annapolis is 50 years older than Williamsburg, giving it time to have at least four names before its present one.

In 1660, the first lot was surveyed and the settlement was named Providence by the Puritans who settled there. Next, it was known as Town of Proctors, in honor of a ship captain by that name. City by the Severn, as it was called next, told where it was situated. Anne Arundel Town, its fourth name, honored the wife of the second Lord Baltimore, Cecil Calvert.

The name that finally stuck was Annapolis, bestowed in 1694 to honor Princess Anne, who later became Queen of England.

From November 1783 to August 1784, Annapolis had the distinction of being capital of the United States. It is also recorded that the colonies' first library was founded in Annapolis.

St. Clement's Island, on the lower Potomac River, is the place where the colonists first dropped anchor in Maryland. History tells that their priest, Father Andrew White, suggested that the island be named after St. Clement. The saint had been martyred by having an anchor fastened around his neck and then cast into the sea.

St. Clement's Island became the property of Thomas Gerard who gave it to his daughter, Elizabeth Gerard Blackiston. Owned by the Blackiston family for more than two centuries, and called Blackiston's Island during that time, the island was renamed "Saint Clement's Island" in 1962 by the Federal Government. Now a 40-foot cross to commemorate the landing marks the island which has dwindled from several hundred acres to around 40 acres at present.

The town we know as Crisfield today was built on a 1663 land grant to John Roach and Benjamin Somers and named Somers Cove. The town was renamed Crisfield to honor the man responsible for bringing the railroad to town shortly after the Civil War.

Much of the town is built on oystershells and, although it is an old town, few old buildings remain because seven large fires within a few decades destroyed major portions of Crisfield.

Dale's Gift was the name men gave to the first settlement on the Virginia Eastern Shore. Sir Thomas Dale sent them there to make salt for the colony in about 1614 or 1616. The men expressed their feelings in this cynical name because they thought it would be miserable, lonely and uncomfortable there.

Four rivers with the name Wicomico flow into Chesapeake Bay: two in Maryland and two in Virginia.

Virginia's Little Wicomico flows into the Bay at Smith Point; the Great Wicomico flows into the Bay just south of it. Both are on the Northern Neck, the peninsula formed by the Potomac and Rappahannock Rivers.

One Maryland Wicomico flows into the Potomac between St. Mary's and Charles counties; the other flows through Salisbury and into Tangier Sound on the Eastern Shore.

Wicomico is a nice name, but why four of them?

From 1669 to 1795, an Eastern Shore town, now called Hadlock, was called T B. It was named T B, so the story goes, because Thomas Bell burned his initials into shingles with a branding iron and nailed them to trees to mark his property there.

A bivalve is a mollusk, such as an oyster, having a shell consisting of two hinged parts. Bivalve is also a Maryland town on the east bank of the Nanticoke River.

Other Bay towns have names honoring the oyster. One is Oyster, Virginia, while the Pocomoke River boasts two oyster-ish towns—Oystershell and Shelltown.

John Smith called Newport News, Point Hope. But, as early as 1619, everyone else knew Point Hope as Newport News as we still do today, more than 350 years later.

The town was renamed after Capt. Christopher Newport who made five trips to Jamestown from England between 1607 and 1619, bringing news and provisions from home.

Frenchtown, once a thriving steamboat terminus on the Elk River, was originally called Transtown, a Swedish name meaning crane, because of the many cranes seen in the marshes. The name changed to Frenchtown when a group of French Acadians, who were banished from Nova Scotia, moved there in 1755. No buildings remain in Frenchtown today.

The name of Rockawalkin, a town on the Eastern Shore, probably evolved from an Indian word. But natives like to tell the following story:

They say an old man named Rock lived in the village. He always rode a bicycle or drove a horse and buggy, but he never walked. On a hot day, a group of men were sitting in the shade. One looked up and exclaimed, "Look, here come old Rock a'walkin'." The event was so momentous that the town was named after it.

Royal Oak was shown on maps made before 1812, so it cannot be true, as some say, that the town got its name from a cannonball shot into an oak tree from a Royal Navy ship during the War of 1812. Perhaps the name came from a royal oak seedling brought from England and planted there.

For a time, Royal Oak was famous because it was touted as the healthiest place in the United States, according to an unpublished federal government agency survey. This turned out to be a fictitious boast made up by a local newspaper editor to make a real estate advertisement more attractive.

Two major explanations circulate as to the origin of the name of Wolf Trap Light.

One says that the land to the west of it, a peninsula between the Piankatank River and Mobjack Bay, was once a famous place to catch wolverines.

Another account tells that a British ship, the HMS *Wolf*, went hard aground on the treacherous shoal, hence the name Wolf Trap.

A settlement grew up at the mouth of the Susquehanna River. First known as Harmer's Town, it then became Stockett's Town and later was called Lower Susquehanna Ferry when a ferry was established there in 1695.

In 1782, the Marquis de Lafayette is said to have looked down over the town as he rode along the Post Road. Commenting that it was a havre de grace, or charming harbor, the town has since been called Havre de Grace.

Hooper and Taylors Islands were both named after early settlers. Hooper was named for Henry Hooper who was granted 100 acres on the island by patent from Lord Calvert in 1667. Taylors Island gained its name from Thomas Taylor who owned land there in the 1600's.

Hooper Strait, between Hooper Island and Bloodsworth Island, was named Limbo by John Smith. When his boat was driven there by a storm, Smith's men had to repair the boat's tattered sails with their shirts.

———

Secretary Creek and the town of Secretary are both named after Henry Sewall, secretary to the Colony of Maryland under Charles Calvert. He owned 2,000 acres on the Choptank River.

———

Plaindealing Creek got its name from the Indians who went to that location to trade with the Quakers. Because the Indians considered the Quakers honest and fair traders, they referred to them as plaindealers.

———

Vienna, Maryland, was not named after the famous European capital of the same name. It is a corruption of Vinnacokasimmon, chief of the Indians whose village originally occupied the site of the town on the Nanticoke.

———

Port Tobacco seems aptly named because of its commerce. It was designated an Official Tobacco Crown Inspection and Tax Collection Port and hence exported considerable tobacco.

Surprisingly, it was not named because of this function, but rather for the Indian town called Potobac, or Potopaco, which occupied the site first.

———

Several main schools of thought divide people who tell how the Tred Avon River got its name. One faction says the river was known as Thread Haven because English merchant ships brought thread, cordage and ropes up the river to Oxford to trade for tobacco. Thread Haven evolved into Tred Avon.

Another faction claims the river was originally known as Third Haven because it was the third haven off the Choptank after Harris and Broad Creeks. This eventually was contracted to Tred Avon.

Another variation of how the river was named is that Avon was a common name for rivers and streams in England. So the English settlers quite naturally referred to the Avon in the first place.

Some have noted that a channel might be called the thread of a river. Then, too, clerks, who spelled phonetically in early days, might have spelled thread as thredde, tred, thrid, or threed.

To add to this confusion, on a 1660 patent, the river was called Tiedhaven; on a 1669 ordinance, Trudhaven; on a 1683 tract, Tredaven; and on a 1776 map, Treavon.

———

Port Deposit, on the Susquehanna River, actually does serve as a port of deposit. The river rapids there cause goods to be transshipped between the river and coastal trade.

Punch Island Creek (near James and Taylors Islands) was so named because it was reputed to be a landing place for bootleggers during Prohibition.

_____

Two John's Landing, on the Choptank River, is named after two men named John who lived there. The men, who weighed more than 300 pounds each, had been a vaudeville team in the 1880's.

_____

Pocomoke City was one of the first Worcester County settlements. Through the years the town has had five different names: Stevens Ferry, Meeting House Landing, Warehouse Landing, Newtown, and finally Pocomoke City, on the river of the same name.

_____

Patuxent is said to be an Indian name meaning "the place where tobacco grows."

_____

Onancock meant "foggy place" in the Algonquin language. The town of Onancock was established as a port of entry for Accomack and Northampton Counties in the 1600's.

_____

The legend of Stingray Point dates all the way back to John Smith's voyage in 1607, when his boat went aground there.

While Smith was waiting for the tide to refloat his boat, he amused himself by spearing fish with his sword. A ray he caught stung his arm, which then swelled terribly. Thinking he would die, Smith chose his prospective burial place on shore, naming it Stingray. However, the expedition's good doctor applied medicine to the sting, Smith recovered miraculously and was able to cook and eat the stingray for supper.

_____

Broad Creek was the name of Kent Island's first town, possibly the first town on Maryland's Eastern Shore. It became Lankford, then Kent Island, and eventually Stevensville, by which it is known today.

_____

Tappahannock was an Indian word, meaning "on the rising water." This town on the Rappahannock River was designated a port of entry in 1680 and some time in its early years was called Hobbs Hole.

Discovering the Bay Today

Museums and Historic Sites

Many museums have been established around the Bay to preserve evidence of times past. Some of the collections are large, some small. Some are diversified while others are dedicated to a single subject.

A few of these museums have been established with substantial grants of money or the backing of large foundations. Others have sprung up through efforts of the local populace which has donated items grown valuable after years in an attic or barn.

Historic sites around the Bay also offer glimpses of our heritage. Festivals and local celebrations provide another aspect of Bay Country culture. Bay buffs may enjoy a wide range of specialties at all seasons of the year.

A sampling of museums and historic spots follows. The list is arranged so you can follow it from north to south, first in Maryland, then in Virginia, with western shore locations preceding eastern shore sites. Potomac River locations begin in Washington, D.C., and continue to the Bay. Virginia sites on the river are enumerated before Maryland ones.

Festivals occur year-around, so they are listed in calendar order with Virginia events preceding Maryland ones. Since events may change dates slightly from year to year, do check in advance for time, place and possible admission charges. Advance inquiry may save visitors disappointment, especially if one is traveling from afar.

———

In the Baltimore area several sites of special interest may be visited.

Fort McHenry, on the Patapsco River, became famous by withstanding the 25-hour bombardment by British naval forces during which Francis Scott Key was inspired to write "The Star-Spangled Banner." The fort is open daily, 8 a.m. to 8 p.m. from June through Labor Day, and from 9 a.m. to 5 p.m. the rest of the year.

The Maryland Historical Society houses a museum pertaining to the history of the entire state. The marine display, primarily M.V. Brewington's personal collection, relates particularly to Chesapeake Bay and Bay boats. Located at 201 Monument St., the museum is open Tuesday through Saturday, 11 a.m. to 4 p.m.

The Shot Tower, built in 1829 for the production of shot, is the only one of its kind remaining in America. Located at Fayette Street and Front Street.

The Star-Spangled Banner Flag House was the home of Mary Pickersgill. She gained fame by making the huge flag that inspired Key to write the national anthem. Located at 844 East Pratt Street. Open Tuesday through Saturday, 10 a.m. to 4 p.m.; on Sundays from 2 to 4:30 p.m.

At Pier 1 on Pratt Street, the U.S. Frigate *Constellation* may be visited. Launched in Baltimore in 1797 and famous as the first ship of the U.S. Navy, it is open Monday through Saturday, 10 a.m. to 4 p.m.; on Sundays from noon to 5 p.m.

Baltimore has its Washington Monument, too, located at Mt. Vernon Place. The monument contains exhibits showing Washington's association with Baltimore. Open Friday through Tuesday, 10:30 a.m. to 4 p.m.

おそら

In Druid Hill Park, the Maryland Museum of Natural History is administered by the Natural History Society of Maryland. Open April to October, Wednesday through Sunday, 10 a.m. to 5 p.m.

———

Chief focus in Anne Arundel County is Maryland's capital city, Annapolis. The State House may be visited daily from 9 a.m. to 5 p.m. and is a good place to begin a tour of old Annapolis. The building, begun in 1772, is the oldest state capitol still in legislative use and has the distinction of having served briefly as our nation's capitol. The Continental Congress met there in the Old Senate Chamber and George Washington resigned his commission as Commander-in-chief of the Army on Dec. 23, 1783.

The United States Naval Academy Museum on the Academy grounds is devoted to mementoes of naval history. Because Chesapeake Bay was a center of naval activity during the War of 1812, its collection of John Paul Jones memorabilia and even more navy memorabilia offers Bay buffs much of interest here. Open to the public Tuesday through Saturday, 9 a.m. to 5 p.m.; Sundays, 11 a.m. to 5 p.m.

A new museum worth visiting, the Annapolis Naval Historical Wax Museum, dramatically presents naval history and episodes from colonial Maryland. See the realistically staged scene of the 1776 *Turtle*, first operational submarine; Marylander Matthew Henson and an Eskimo guide as they accompanied Peary on his 1909 trek to the North Pole. View other tableaux covering Maryland history from 1633 to the present, at this City Dock location.

Open seven days a week year-around (except Christmas). Hours, May through October, 9 a.m. to 9 p.m.; November through April, 9 a.m. to 6 p.m.

For the historically-inclined, the Hall of Records on St. John's College campus, Annapolis, is open for public use. State archives and documents are available Monday through Saturday, 8:30 a.m. to 4:30 p.m.

On South River, a short distance from Annapolis, is London Town Publik House, recently restored. The inn and port have been used since colonial times. Located at Edgewater, the museum is open daily, 10 a.m. to 4 p.m.

———

Calvert Marine Museum in Solomons is preparing to move into larger quarters in the former Solomons Elementary School. The waterfront site will permit expansion of exhibits relating to the maritime history of the area. Mementoes of old-time boatbuilding, unique fossil finds, trailboard carving and other displays may be seen Saturdays and Sundays, 1 to 5 p.m. and at other times by special arrangement.

———

The Harry Lundeberg School of Seamanship, at Piney Point, Md., is a unique establishment on the lower Potomac. It is essentially the seafarers' union school where young men prepare for careers at sea. Utilized during instruction are the several vessels comprising the school's fleet. The craft are a sort of living museum, crowned by the famed *Manitou.* This handsome yawl was sailed by the late President John F. Kennedy while he was in office.

Visitors are usually welcome one Sunday each month. Write for details and admission particulars.

W.R. (Ruby) Dixon, foreman; Frank Dare, Charles Elliott, Joe Johnson, Leroy (Pepper) Langley, Olin (Bill) Joy, and Ed Selby, seven men who helped build the *Manitou* in the Solomons, Md., yard of M.M. Davis and Son in the 1930's, stand beneath her when she was raised recently for maintenance.

Manitou is now part of the fleet at the Lundeberg School of Seamanship, at Piney Point, Md. She was once owned by the U.S. Coast Guard and was frequently sailed by the late President John F. Kennedy. Bob Barton

St. Mary's City, in Maryland's Mother County of St. Marys, is the location of the first Maryland State House, erected in 1676. The present building is a 1934 reconstruction of the original, open daily from 10 a.m. to 5 p.m., May through October. Hours are 10 a.m. to 4 p.m. from November through April.

Nearby is Trinity Episcopal Church, built in 1829 from bricks of the original State House before the capital was moved to Annapolis.

The "Freedom of Conscience" monument, near St. Mary's College campus, was erected in 1934 in celebration of Maryland's tercentenary. It symbolizes the religious freedom on which the state was founded.

Also in St. Mary's City is a tall obelisk, the Leonard Calvert monument, standing near Trinity Church. It marks the site of the mulberry tree under which it is said the first colonists assembled to establish a government.

Located on the Patuxent River near Hollywood is another St. Marys County landmark. Sotterley, built in 1730, is maintained as a working plantation and remains open June through October daily, from 11 a.m. to 5 p.m.

Point Lookout State Park, Scotland, Md., is at the Potomac's confluence with the Bay. The park contains remains of a Civil War prison camp and a monument to those who died there. Open daily, 8 a.m. to 10 p.m.

A unique Eastern Shore location is the Chesapeake and Delaware Canal Museum, established in what was the boiler room of the old, gray stone pump house for the Chesapeake City lock which has no present use. The building houses the old waterwheel, 38 feet in diameter and 10 feet wide, which could lift 1,200,000 gallons of water into the lock every hour. Other objects from the canal's history and fossils dug from its banks are also on display.

A museum-in-the-making is located at Turner's Creek in Kent County. Several old buildings have been moved to the museum grounds which include the site of a very early settlement which has since disappeared. These buildings, when renovated, will form the nucleus of a reconstructed village. A new building will display old farming equipment used in Kent County.

The museum may be reached by walking up the hill from the county landing in Turner's Creek, or by driving north on Route 448 from Kennedyville.

The Wye Oak is the only one-tree state forest in the United States, and rates as something special to visit. The tree is approximately 400 years old, 50 feet in circumference and 95 feet tall. The branches spread 165 feet.

Since 1909, when this white oak was declared the largest specimen of its kind in the eastern United States, the tree has been trimmed, fertilized and braced to preserve its good health.

The Wye Oak is the State Tree of Maryland, and it is the only one-tree state forest in the United States. Maryland Department of Economic and Community Development

Seedlings from the tree have been raised by the State Forest Service and sold to people who wished to own their own Wye Oak.

The Wye Oak is located next to State Highway 622, in Wye Mills, Talbot County, Md.

The Chesapeake Bay Maritime Museum, in St. Michaels, Md., has a large collection of indigenous Bay boats, watermen's tools and a new building devoted to waterfowling on Chesapeake Bay. The screwpile lighthouse from Hooper Strait is preserved here, as is a lightship. An aquarium filled with Bay marine life is on the grounds.

The museum is open from 10 a.m. to 5 p.m. in the summer and 10 a.m. to 4 p.m. in winter, except Mondays and Christmas. When Monday is a holiday, the museum remains open.

The St. Mary's Square Museum, in St. Michaels, is located a few blocks from the harbor in the town's residential district. The museum building is itself a museum—a small house constructed of hand-hewn

This building, which will house waterfowl exhibits, is a recent addition to the Chesapeake Bay Maritime Museum, at St. Michaels. Anne M. Hays

half-timbers in the 17th century. Life during the colonial and other historic periods in St. Michaels is depicted in the items displayed inside.

The museum is open April through September on Fridays, Saturdays and Sundays, from 10 a.m. to 4 p.m. and on other days by request.

The Oxford Museum is located across from the park in Oxford, a short walk from the docks. All of its exhibits relate to the early history of Oxford. A 1707 map of the town is on display. The collection of shipwright's tools is of particular interest. The museum is open Friday, Saturday and Sunday, 2 to 5 p.m., and by special arrangement at other times.

Talbot County Courthouse in Easton is a 1794 structure on whose grounds the Talbot Resolves were adopted. These sentiments were later incorporated into the Declaration of Independence. Open Monday through Friday, 8:30 a.m. to 4 p.m.

In Somerset County, Rehobeth Presbyterian Church is located at Rehobeth on the Pocomoke River. The church was founded by Francis Makemie, a founder of Presbyterianism on the Eastern Shore. The church's exterior, dating to 1706, is unaltered. Open continuously.

Items in everyday use during the 1800's are the principal display in the Julia A. Purnell Museum in Snow Hill, on the Pocomoke River. Many of the items exhibited belonged to Mrs. Purnell, whose life spanned the 100 years from 1843 to 1943. A collection of framed quotes telling of things unique to that period and remembered by Mrs. Purnell is of special interest. The museum is open Sundays, from 1 to 5 p.m.

Tidewater Potomac extends to Washington, D.C., 90 miles from the Bay. Much of maritime interest may be found in our Nation's Capital and a few of the historic and unique locations are described briefly.

The U.S. Navy Memorial Museum is housed in Building No. 76, Washington Navy Yard. All major caliber guns ever produced for the U.S. Navy were processed here. Included among many exhibits are the late President John F. Kennedy's ship model collection, Paul Revere's commission as a messenger and countless other artifacts from 1775 to the present. Open Monday through Saturday, from 9 a.m. to 4 p.m. Closed Sunday. Summer hours are weekdays, 9 a.m. to 4 p.m.; Saturday and Sunday, 10 a.m. to 5 p.m.

The Smithsonian Institution is big enough to house just about everything. Visitors sometimes overlook two top-notch maritime collections: the Hall of American Merchant Shipping and the Hall of the Armed Forces of the U.S., with its naval history exhibits. Models of warships from colonial days to modern times, the evolution of vessels like fishing, cargo and passenger ships and much more are included.

Here also is America's oldest man-of-war, built in just two months. It successfully delayed the British on Lake Champlain, thereby leading to eventual victory at Saratoga, in 1777.

Truxtun-Decatur Naval Museum, 1610 H. Street, N.W., is situated in small quarters just off Lafayette Square. The museum is named for Commodore Thomas Truxtun, a distinguished officer in our war with France, in 1798-1800, and for Commodore Stephen Decatur, Jr., remembered as hero of the war with Tripoli. Included are all types of naval and maritime materials illustrating the U.S. Navy from Revolutionary War days to the present. Open daily except Monday, 10:30 a.m. to 4 p.m.

Moored in the Washington Channel, along the East Potomac Park seawall, is the Lightship *Chesapeake*. Now called the National Park Service Lightship for Environmental Awareness, the *Chesapeake* had a distinguished career as part of the Lighthouse Service. The bright red lightship gave 40 years of dedicated service marking harbor approaches, gathering meteorological data and otherwise serving her country.

Now Sea Scouts man the ship and visitors are welcome from 1 to 4 p.m. on Saturday and Sunday. Summer visiting hours, June to September, are Tuesday, Thursday, Saturday and Sunday, from 1 to 5 p.m.

————

Across the Potomac from the Nation's Capital lies Arlington, once part of the original District of Columbia. It was returned to Virginia in 1846.

Visit Arlington House, also known as the Lee-Custis Mansion, once the home of Gen. Robert E. Lee. A portion of the original estate became Arlington National Cemetery. Open daily, 9:30 a.m. to 4:30 p.m., October through March; 9:30 a.m. to 6 p.m., April through September.

Other Arlington sites near Memorial Bridge are the Iwo Jima War Memorial and the Netherlands Carillon Tower. At the Iwo Jima statue the flag flies 24 hours a day in tribute to U.S. Marines in World War II. Each Tuesday evening during the summer impressive military ceremonies are held at the memorial.

The Netherlands Carillon Tower was given by the Dutch people in appreciation of American wartime and postwar aid. Summertime bell concerts are held at 3 p.m. on Sundays.

————

In Old Town Alexandria, begin at Ramsay House Visitors Center, where the town's first Lord Mayor once lived. Visitors may see a color film about the city and choose which sites to explore on a pleasant walking tour a few blocks from docks along the Potomac.

The river's shores are shrouded in history, some spots well-known, others of specialized interest. After Mount Vernon, with its grand view down the Potomac, stop at Quantico, the U.S. Marine Corps Base. Here the U.S. Marine Corps Museum depicts the corps' history from 1775 to the present. Open Monday through Friday, from 9 a.m. to 6 p.m., Saturdays, 9 a.m. to 5 p.m., and Sundays and holidays, from 12 noon to 4 p.m. Closed New Year's and Christmas.

Occoquan lies south of Gunston Hall and its neighboring Mount Vernon. Once Occoquan was a port and marinas still line its waterfront. The Mill House, built before 1800, houses a museum. Open Sundays, from 1 to 5 p.m.

Near Colonial Beach, situated in Westmoreland County and long known as a Potomac resort, are two historic sites. Stratford Hall is the ancestral home of the Lees of Virginia and Wakefield is now referred to as the George Washington National Birthplace.

Coan Wharf on the Coan River, once was a seaport town of entry, so designated in 1680. Until the 1930's, a cable ferry ran across a Coan tributary to Bundick's.

On the Potomac's Maryland shore, a short distance below Washington, D.C., stands Fort Washington. Now a Military Historical Park, the fort, built between 1814 and 1824, replaced an earlier one destroyed during the War of 1812. See the drawbridge and batteries. Open daily year-round. The park museum is open June 1 to Labor Day; weekends and holidays the remainder of the year.

In Charles County, Md., visit Gen. Smallwood's Retreat, now a state park. Originally it was the home of the Revolutionary War patriot and Governor of Maryland. Open daily, 10 a.m. to 6 p.m.

Farther down the Potomac, near Chapel Point and Pope's Creek, John Wilkes Booth tried to cross the river after hiding out in Surrattsville (now called Clinton, Md.) following his assassination of President Abraham Lincoln.

Virginia museums and historical sites are listed next with Western Shore locations preceding Eastern Shore spots.

In Fredericksburg, once a Rappahannock River port, is the Monroe Law Office. James Monroe practiced law there several years before he became president of the United States.

Old Port Royal was one of the principal shipping points on the Rappahannock in colonial times. Nearby the assassin of President Lincoln, John Wilkes Booth, met his miserable end. He died in a barn in the area just 12 days after he shot Lincoln.

Near Weems stands Christ Church, burial place of Robert (King) Carter of colonial fame. The church, built in 1732, has walls over three feet thick and the structure has never been altered in over 200 years.

Near Gloucester is Belroi, birthplace of Dr. Walter Reed, of the U.S. Army. He was the first man to prove that yellow fever is conveyed by mosquitoes.

Richmond, located at the fall line of the James River, has been the state capital since 1779. One of its famous buildings is the Capitol, designed by Thomas Jefferson after the Maison Carrée, at Nîmes, France.

Richmond's Hollywood Cemetery is the resting place of two presidents, James Monroe and John Tyler. Here also is the grave of Commodore Matthew Fontaine Maury, the great naval scientist who plotted the currents of the Atlantic Ocean.

At Surry, on the James' south shore, stands Virginia's first commercial nuclear facility. Open Monday through Friday, 10 a.m. to 4 p.m.; Sunday, from 1 to 6 p.m.

The James River Plantations, all historic sites dating back to colonial times, are scattered along both shores of the James River. Among them are Appomattox Manor, near Hopewell (not open to the public), where General U.S. Grant headquartered for a time. Plantations usually open to the public include Brandon, Shirley, Berkeley, Carter's Grove and several others of considerable charm and interest. At Berkeley, the first official Thanksgiving Day was celebrated and in recent years the occasion has been revived.

———

The triangle of Jamestown, Williamsburg and Yorktown, lying between the James and the York, comprise one of our country's most

Comparing the three boats that carried 104 colonists to Jamestown with the visitors strolling on the dock emphasizes how small the boats were for that long ocean voyage from England. Jamestown Foundation

historic areas. Information centers at each location can supply much helpful and fascinating detail for visitors, such as visiting hours and special interest areas.

In Jamestown, look for the ancient tower, hardly more than a ruin, dating back to 1639. This site is a reminder that Jamestown was capital of Virginia for 92 years. Here the first representative legislative assembly of the New World met in 1619.

Also at Jamestown, see replicas of the three original ships that brought the first colonists to these shores.

Williamsburg, capital of Virginia from 1699 to 1779, lives in restoration as it looked during the 18th century when the colonies were increasingly in ferment. Visit the handsome Governor's Palace where the original structure was used as a hospital for men wounded at Yorktown. See the Storehouse for arms and ammunition for the colony, many craft shops, Wythe House, the home of Thomas Jefferson's law professor and the Capitol, reconstructed after its two predecessors were burned. And there's so much more to explore.

Yorktown, usually remembered for its importance in the Revolutionary War, actually was under siege during the Civil War too. View the Siege Line Lookout from the Yorktown Center and gaze out toward Chesapeake Bay where the French fleet blockaded the British in Yorktown, in 1781. See old cannon, fortifications, a partially reconstructed British frigate and dioramas of battle scenes.

Beyond the historical colonial triangle at the end of the peninsula is the location of both Hampton and Newport News. Across Hampton Roads lies Norfolk, situated across the Elizabeth River from Portsmouth. Completing the circle of cities at Chesapeake Bay's southern end are Virginia Beach and the city of Chesapeake.

Here again, the recommended course for visitors is to seek information centers and choose from the numerous interesting locations in the area.

Hampton, called Kecoughtan by the Indians, was the scene of a trading post set up in 1630 by William Claiborne who also traded on Kent Island, Maryland, where he made history.

Also at Hampton is Fort Monroe, begun in 1819, commanding the entrance to Hampton Roads. It is the location of the Casemate Museum commemorating the captivity of a famous Indian chief and of Jefferson Davis, Confederate president.

At Hampton Institute, the college museum contains an important collection of American Indian exhibits.

Other Hampton sites include the Lightship *Hampton*, a floating maritime museum and the Kenneth E. Rice Memorial Museum. You may dig your own fossils from the pit at this museum, located just off Fox

Creek Road on Harris Creek Road. Open weekdays, 9:30 a.m. to 5:30 p.m.; Sundays, 2 to 6 p.m.

———

In Newport News, be sure to see one of the world's great marine museums. The Mariners Museum, in an 80-acre park, has a huge collection of figureheads and the remarkable exhibition of the Crabtree Collection of miniature handcrafted ships. A display of submarine development and other maritime items too numerous to mention here are also displayed. Open Monday through Saturday, 9 a.m. to 5 p.m.; Sunday, 12 noon to 5 p.m. Closed Christmas Day.

Natural history of the region, including a live animal area, may be seen at Peninsula Junior Nature Museum and Planetarium. Open Tuesday through Saturday, 9 a.m. to 5 p.m.; Sunday, 2 to 5 p.m.

———

At Portsmouth is the Naval History Museum with emphasis on the history of the U.S. Navy. Next to it is the Coast Guard Museum, housed in a former Coast Guard lightship. Both open Tuesday through Saturday and holidays, from 10 a.m. to 5 p.m.; open Sunday, from 2 to 5 p.m.

———

See also the Norfolk Naval Shipyard, dating from 1767. Here was built the first armored warship, the *Merrimack*. Tours arranged Monday through Saturday.

The view of modern Norfolk makes it difficult to believe that it was settled in 1682, totally destroyed in 1776 and rebuilt. During the Civil War it became the chief naval station of the Confederacy.

Located in the old city courthouse is the Gen. Douglas MacArthur Memorial, where war souvenirs and mementoes are on display. Open Monday through Saturday, 10 a.m. to 5 p.m.; Sunday, 11 a.m. to 5 p.m. Closed New Year's Day and Christmas.

Guided boat tours are offered at Norfolk "Gardens-by-the-Sea," beautiful with azalea, camellia and rhododendron gardens surrounding lakes in the park. Tours daily, 10 a.m. to 6 p.m., April through October.

Norfolk Naval Station tours include visits to the Naval Air Station and submarine piers. Tours at intervals, 10:30 a.m. to 2:30 p.m., April 1 to Oct. 15.

———

Chesapeake, now a city, is a consolidation of the ancient city of South Norfolk and the county of Norfolk. It extends from the northern North Carolina border to the city limits of Virginia Beach, Norfolk and Portsmouth.

The Great Dismal Swamp lies in this area and extends into North Carolina. In 1763, George Washington explored there and organized a company which planned to drain the area for farmland. The Intra-coastal Waterway passes through the Swamp and tours of the area, including Lake Drummond within the Swamp, may be arranged. Write Pefley Enterprises, 5717 Sellger Drive, Norfolk, Va. 23502.

East of Norfolk lies the city of Virginia Beach, with Cape Henry at its tip. Visit the great cross marking the landing of the first permanent English settlers before they established Jamestown. The old brick light-house dates back to 1791.

The unique Chesapeake Bay Bridge-Tunnel's southern terminus is in Virginia Beach, not far from the Adam Thoroughgood House, a little 17th century brick house of great charm. Open Monday through Satur-day, 10 a.m. to 5 p.m.; Sunday from 11 a.m. to 6 p.m., April 1 through Thanksgiving. Longer hours in summer.

North of the mouth of Chesapeake Bay, Virginia's eastern shore occupies the tip of the Delmarva Peninsula.

Accomac, county seat of Accomack County is believed to have more restored colonial buildings than any other town of its size.

Stop in at the museum of the Eastern Shore of Virginia Historical Society, located on Kerr Place in Onancock. Open from April 1 to November 30.

At Eastville, see the Debtors' Prison behind the old courthouse, built about 1731. From the courthouse entrance, the Declaration of Inde-pendence was read in August 1776.

Festivals and Local Celebrations

Virginia festivals and local celebrations are listed in calender order.

January
Open House at Stratford Hall—Stratford.
From 7 to 9 p.m., the Westmoreland County home of Gen. Robert E. Lee opens in honor of his birthday. No admission charge.

February
Open House at Mount Vernon.
Honoring the birthday of George Washington, the third Monday in February. No admis-sion charge.

April
Annual Daffodil Show of Garden Club of Virginia—Gloucester.
Although the seafood industry and marine biological research are most often associated with this county, Gloucester has many acres of daffodils that draw visitors from great distances.

International Azalea Festival—Norfolk.
This port city turns its attention from sea to land when azaleas bloom in the famous "Gardens-by-the-Sea." Event honors the North Atlantic Treaty Organization's Atlantic Headquarters in Norfolk.

Art and Craft Show—Accomac, Old Courthouse Green.
Local Eastern Shore artists demonstrate such dying arts as duck carving and wood sculpture.

Cape Henry Day—Cape Henry.
The Order of Cape Henry, 1607, commemorates in 1975 the 368th anniversary of the landing of the first permanent English-speaking settlers at Cape Henry. The ceremonies are of a religious nature. The public is invited to the Cross within the grounds of Fort Story, Virginia.

May
Annual Virginia Salt Water Fishing Tournament—Virginia Beach.
Rod and reel competition for fish ranging from spot to shark, with citations for prize catch.

Jamestown Day—Jamestown.
Commemoration ceremonies celebrate the arrival of the colonists of America's first permanent English settlement, at Jamestown, on May 13, 1607. (Ceremonies on second Sunday of May.)

Prelude to Independence—Williamsburg.
Colonial Williamsburg annually commemorates the period between May 15 and July 4, 1776, when many historic events occurred in Williamsburg immediately before the American War for Independence.

Annual Potomac River Festival—Colonial Beach.
Three days of parades, contests, music and celebration to usher in summer at this resort town on the Potomac.

July
Open House at Stratford Hall—Stratford.
Honors the only two brothers to sign the Declaration of Independence: Richard Henry Lee and Francis Lightfoot Lee.

October
Annual Fredericksburg Dog Mart—Fredericksburg.
An event that began in 1698, when early colonists traded their dogs for the Indians' furs and gold nuggets. Unique parade, dog show and auction, hog calling, fox horn blowing.

Yorktown Day—Yorktown.
Observance of the day the American War for Independence ended with surrender of Cornwallis at Yorktown, October 19, 1781.

November
Annual Oyster Festival—Urbanna.
Parade, antique car show and other festivities mark the season for Virginia oyster harvest at this Rappahannock River town.

Maryland's list of local celebrations and festivals follows:

January
Ratification Day—Annapolis.
Commemorates the anniversary of the Ratification of the Treaty of Paris, which officially ended the Revolutionary War.

February
Annual Cambridge Outdoor Show—Cambridge.
Attend the Muskrat Skinning National Championship.

March

Maryland Day—Baltimore and St. Mary's City.

Ceremonies in Baltimore celebrate the anniversary of Maryland's founding. The state holiday commemorates the landing of settlers in 1634 at St. Clement's Island. At St. Mary's City a symbolic legislative session is held in the State House of 1676.

April

Annual Day in Oxford.

Tour of this charming Eastern Shore village, once the home of Revolutionary War figures. Write for information.

World Championship Wildfowl Carving Competition—Salisbury.

Visitors to this extraordinary assemblage of wood-carvers and their crafts may see decorative decoys, lifesize and miniature wildfowl. In all, nearly one thousand skillfully carved and expertly painted replicas of many kinds of waterfowl, songbirds, game birds and birds of prey will be on view after judging and awarding of prizes. Write to Wildfowl Carving Competition, Salisbury, Md., for details.

May

Colonial Charlestown Fair—Charlestown.

A recreation of a 1744 fair. Colonial and modern crafts demonstrated and sold. 3rd Maryland Regiment of Revolution performs.

Cavalier Days in Calvert County—Prince Frederick.

1780's fair atmosphere. Tobacco auction, dancing, games, crafts, music, local food specialities.

Pocomoke River/Snow Hill Water Festival—Snow Hill.

Riverside festival with canoe races, arts and crafts, music, games, auction, fishing contest, dancing, tours of historic buildings. Crabcakes, oysters and barbequed chicken available for the hungry.

Chestertown Tea Party Festival—Chestertown.

The town's 1774 Tea Party, similar to Boston's but not so famous, is reenacted as part of two days of colonial Eastern Shore style activities. Parades, exhibits, tours, dancing, boat races, etc.

U.S. Naval Academy Commissioning Week—Annapolis.

Athletic events, parades and other ceremonies over a six-day period prior to graduation and commissioning exercises.

June

Delmarva Chicken Festival—A different Eastern Shore site each year.

Food, fun and frolic for all ages are promised. Activities center around Delmarva Chicken Cooking Contest.

Confederates Day—Scotland.

An afternoon of activities to honor the Confederate prisoners who died at the prisoner of war camp at Point Lookout. The area is now a state park.

Flag Day Celebration—Baltimore.

Held at Ft. McHenry where the "star spangled banner" of our national anthem flew. Three hours of entertainment by drill teams and military bands.

Pocomoke Cypress Festival—Pocomoke City.

Raft race on the river. Bands and other entertainment ashore.

July

Cambridge Power Boat Regatta Classic (Inboard)—Cambridge.

One of the oldest power boat regattas in the country. Races for hydroplanes, runabouts and Jersey speed skiffs. Corn roast and crab feast.

J. Millard Tawes Crab and Clam Bake—Crisfield.
A get-together for the purpose of indulging in eating good things like steamed crabs, corn on the cob, fresh fried fish, clams, etc.

North East Water Festival—North East.
State Sculling Championship, water-oriented displays, boat parade, fish fry and more.

August
Wheat Threshing, Steam and Gas Engine Show—Denton/Federalsburg.
See how the harvesting was done on the Eastern Shore years ago. Also exhibits of sawmilling, shingle sawing, rock crushing, broommaking and blacksmithing.

Summer Candlelight Tour—Edgewater.
Evening tours of London Town Publik House and gardens. The house is a restored, 18th century ferry tavern.

September
National Hard Crab Derby and Fair—Crisfield.
The crab derby is the main event, but the three-day fair also includes crab cooking and

Crab Derby

picking contests, boat docking competition, fireworks, band concerts and a carnival with rides, games and refreshments.

Solomons Arts and Crafts Festival—Solomons.
Held at the Calvert Marine Museum, artisans will demonstrate and sell their crafts. Seafood featured at refreshment stands.

Labor Day Skipjack Races—Deal Island.
Skipjacks take a day off from dredging for oysters for a traditional day of racing. Also races for other classes of sailboats and other activities.

Candlelight Walking Tour of Chestertown—Chestertown.
Private homes of the 18th, 19th and 20th century open for one evening of touring by candlelight.

Dorchester Showcase—Cambridge.
Tours of historic sites in the county, arts, crafts, music, dancing and Eastern Shore food also featured.

St. Clement's Island Blessing of the Fleet—Colton Point.
One-day celebration on St. Clement's Island, with historic pageant commemorating first landing place of the Maryland colonists in the *Ark* and the *Dove*. Entertainment and Southern Maryland seafood.

October

Wildfowl Carving and Art Exhibition—Salisbury.
Old decoy displays. Contemporary carvers and artists show work.
Wildfowl related articles for sale.

Classic yachts tied up where they could be seen from shore before they paraded during the St. Michaels Days celebration. Anne M. Hays

Olde Princess Anne Days—Princess Anne.
Tours of historic homes and churches. Candlelight tour of the Teakle Mansion on Saturday night.

Patuxent River Appreciation Days—Solomons.
Opportunity to tour both the Calvert Marine Museum and the Chesapeake Biological Laboratory. Exhibits and demonstrations having to do with history and economic importance of Patuxent River.

St. Mary's County Oyster Festival and National Oyster Shucking Championships—
Leonardtown.
St. Mary's County Fairgrounds is setting for entertainment, music and films. Oysters
served in every style.

Chesapeake Appreciation Days—Sandy Point State Park.
The Skipjack races are the focal point of two days dedicated to Bay oriented exhibits and
activities. A chance to taste Maryland seafood prepared in several ways.

November

Tilghman Island Day—Tilghman.
Seafood festival featuring workboat races, boat docking contest and demonstrations of net
making, handtonging and more.

Waterfowl Festival—Easton.
Exhibits of decoys and waterfowl art. Decoy auction. Duck and goose calling contest.

Several cruise boats and passenger ferries operate on the Chesapeake.
Some short excursions to consider are those running between Crisfield and
Ewell, Md., via Tylerton on Smith Island; Crisfield to Rhodes Point; Cris-
field to Tangier, Va.; Reedville to Tangier Island, Va.; and Smith Point,
Va. to Smith Island, Md.

Because schedules change from season to season, we suggest you request current information from such agencies as Maryland's Tourist De-

The *Baltimore*, an 85-foot, turn-of-the-century steam tugboat which has been converted to a
yacht, shown here cruising the Miles River. Anne M. Hays

velopment Office or the Virginia State Travel Service. (See addresses and telephone numbers in Chapter I.)

St. Michaels and Baltimore Harbor—Patriot Cruises, P.O. Box 47, Royal Oak, Md. 21662, 301-745-7031.

Patuxent River—Nature cruise sponsored by the Maryland National Capital Park and Planning Commission, 301-249-9220.

Chesapeake Bay—Charter the brogan *Mustang* from Chesapeake Cruises, based in Annapolis Harbor. P.O. Box 9693, Arnold, Md. 21012, 301-757-3025.

Annapolis Harbor—*The Harbor Queen*, 301-849-5611.

Hampton Roads—Cruises available ranging from mini-trips in Norfolk "Gardens-by-the-Sea" to harbor cruises all around Hampton Roads.

Smith and Tangier Islands—Cruise vessels now operate from both Maryland and Virginia ports.

III. WHO WAS WHO AROUND THE CHESAPEAKE

Indians

Archeological evidence tells us that Indians inhabited the land along the rivers and creeks tributary to the Bay long before the white men arrived from Europe.

Maryland's state archeologist cites evidence that Indians were present in the mid-Chesapeake area as long ago as 8000 B.C.

Radiocarbon dating tests made on oystershells found in Kent County prove that Indians were eating oysters there at least 5,565 years ago.

The Patuxent River valley may have the highest number of fossilized campsites from the prehistoric period in the entire Middle Atlantic area. These sites usually consist of layered oystershells and oval blackened pits filled with charcoal and small bones, indicating an Indian village's location or a well-used campsite.

———

Most of the Indians inhabiting what are now Maryland and Virginia belonged to the Algonquin family of tribes. The Piscataways in southern Maryland and the Nanticokes, Pocomokes, and Assateagues of the Eastern Shore, for example, all had similar speech and customs, indicating a common ancestry. They built dugout canoes, lived in wigwams, wove nets, baskets, and mats and worked with grooved stone axes.

———

The Susquehannocks, an Iroquoian tribe who lived along the Susquehanna River, were large and warlike Indians who so terrified their southern neighbors that these Indians allied themselves with the white men for protection.

Governor Calvert of Maryland first declared the Susquehannocks public enemies, then signed a treaty with them in 1652 giving them all the land between the North East and Susquehanna Rivers.

———

The Indian chief the Jamestown colonists called Powhatan was actually named Wahunsonacock. Powhatan, meaning Falls of the River, was the name of his village, located at the James River Falls near where Richmond now stands. Powhatan's daughter was called Pocahontas, which meant Frisky, but her real name was Matowaka.

Pocahontas married John Rolfe, an English colonist, and died at the age of 21, leaving one son.

Powhatan was a strong leader who had united 200 villages of 30 tribes into a union called the Powhatan Confederacy. The capital of the Powhatan Confederacy was called Werewocomoco and was located on the northeastern shore of the York River. The actual site is not definitely known.

Powhatan was friendly toward the colonists and helped the Jamestown settlers survive the first winter by bringing them corn. But when Powhatan died in 1618, he was succeeded by Opechancanough, who tried to poison the Jamestown wells in 1621 and led an uprising in 1622, killing 350 settlers. In 1644, Opechancanough led another uprising but was captured and killed by a colonist who was supposed to be guarding him. His successor made a treaty with the colonists in 1646, and the Indians were never a strong force again.

The lower Eastern Shore Indians had belonged to the Powhatan Confederacy, but also were united among themselves under the kingship of Debedeavon. He held the title of Ye Emperor of Ye Eastern Shore and King of Ye Great Nussawattocks, and was also called The Laughing King.

Debedeavon saved the Jamestown colony from destruction in 1621 by informing the settlers of Opechancanough's plot to poison their wells with a poisonous herb.

Debedeavon's daughter was named Nandua. She became Empress of the Eastern Shore Indians in 1700. The town of Nandua is on the site of her seat of government.

Kittamaquand was the chief of the Piscataway tribe in southern Maryland when the *Ark* and the *Dove* landed with Calvert's first colonists. He had been chief less than a year, only since the murder of his brother, Wannas.

Kittamaquand's friendship with the colonists did not endear him to his subjects, who were already suspicious that he might have murdered his brother.

Kittamaquand was converted to Christianity in 1640 by Father White, the priest who accompanied the colonists. At his baptism, Leonard Calvert named Kittamaquand Emperor of the Piscataways Charles. Leonard Calvert and Margaret Brent were godparents for Charles' daughter, Mary, who became the first and only American princess when her father was named emperor. Princess Mary married Margaret Brent's brother, Giles Brent. Giles became commander of Kent Island. Giles and Mary lived at Kent Fort until 1647, when they moved to Virginia.

According to the 1970 United States census, only 4,239 Indians lived in Maryland and 4,853 lived in Virginia.

Pirates and Privateers

The first recorded instance of piracy on the Bay occurred in 1610, only three years after the first colonists landed in Jamestown. Thirty "unhallowed creatures" who were sent to trade with the Indians for food in the pinnace *Swallow* became pirates instead.

From then on, until the middle of the 1700's, recorded instances of piracy on Chesapeake Bay and off the Capes are numerous. A sampling follows.

Pirates raided the most important ammunition magazine in the Maryland colony at Mattapany, on the Patuxent River, in 1681. They nearly succeeded in capturing Maryland governor Charles Calvert and the arms stored there before they were turned back.

In 1682, a pirate ship landed a party and sacked two plantation houses at Tindalls Point, at the mouth of the York River.

In 1683, a band of pirates stayed in Accomac for four months while fitting out for a voyage around Cape Horn. They traded their cargo of wines for provisions and naval stores.

Around 1685, a pirate named Roger Makeele and his crew of thirteen men and four women plundered ships on Chesapeake Bay. He lived on the Little Choptank River. Slaughter Creek on that river is named for his lieutenant, who was appropriately named Slaughter. Makeele was undaunted by the presence of a royal warship on the Bay and continued his raids. Most of the gang was eventually captured, however, and hanged. Records do not mention Makeele himself, and he may have escaped.

For unknown reasons, but perhaps to find favor with the colonial governor, three pirates named Davis, Wafer, and Hinson donated £300 to the College of William and Mary in 1692. Along with Davis' negro servant, Cleiss, they had been captured and had spent three years in jail in Jamestown before making the donation.

In 1700, a large pirate ship, *La Paix*, looted ships in the area of the Virginia Capes. The captain was a Frenchman, Louis Guittar. The ship and crew were captured by Francis Nicholson, the governor of Virginia, formerly also the governor of Maryland.

In 1720, two pirates were hanged at Tindalls Point on the York River, and two more were hanged at Urbanna on the Rappahannock River.

———

Because of piracy, it became the practice for merchant ships to travel in convoy with a British man-of-war for protection. When between 50 and 300 ships had gathered at the mouth of the Patuxent and Potomac Rivers and at Point Comfort, they would all sail together. Once offshore, they were relatively safe from attack until they neared the coast of England.

———

Blackbeard, who blockaded the mouth of Chesapeake Bay in 1717, allowing only those who paid tribute to pass, was reputed to be the boldest and most cold-blooded pirate of them all. Perhaps he was, or perhaps he just knew how to project the most piratical image. A colorful or charismatic man we would call him today. He wore his black beard separated into tails, tied with colored ribbons and tucked behind his ears. He wore three pairs of pistols across his chest, plus a cutlass and a knife or two for the close fighting. Just to be sure his men knew who was boss, he was reputed to have mixed gunpowder with rum, set it on fire and drunk it, daring any other to follow his example.

Blackbeard

Blackbeard is said to have always taken only one sailor with him when he went ashore to bury treasure. When the man had dug the hole, put the treasure chest in and half buried it, Blackbeard would knock him on the head, throw him in the hole, and fill it up himself. He supposedly bragged, "Now only the Devil and I know where it is, and I've left one of my men on guard."

As a result of this policy—and perhaps because people wish to believe it—it is rumored that some of Blackbeard's treasure is still buried in various places around the Bay. One such site is the banks of Watts

Creek, a small tributary of the upper Choptank River, which is no longer navigable even for small boats, but which once was possibly a refuge for Blackbeard's ship.

Some of Blackbeard's treasure may also still be buried on Longworth Point, on the east side of the Wicomico River, close to where it joins the Potomac River. Blackbeard, Long Arm, Morgan, Cocklescroft, and other pirates are said to have visited and hidden some of their loot in a house there known as Ocean Haul.

West River and Gibson Island have also been mentioned as possible locations for undiscovered pirate treasure.

Blackbeard and fellow pirate Stede Bonnet are said to have had ships built and outfitted in the early 1700's in Oxford. Blackbeard, it is told, paid off an Oxford shipbuilder by covering a tabletop with gold coins.

A similar story is told about a pirate named Captain Martin, who did business with a shipbuilder named Skillington, in Talbot County. Captain Martin reportedly brought back enough coins from a voyage to cover a tabletop a foot deep with Spanish dollars, some of which he used to pay his bill at the shipyard.

As late as 1750, Spanish gold and silver coins, perhaps part of the pirate booty, were collected in the Talbot County school funds.

Although Blackbeard made occasional forays into Chesapeake Bay, he was even more of a menace off the coast of North Carolina. Even so, the governor of that state would not attempt to arrest him. In 1718, Governor Spotswood of Virginia sent an expedition to capture him, with Lt. Maynard in charge commanding a man-of-war of the Royal Navy. In the fighting, Blackbeard received five pistol wounds and twenty cutlass wounds before he fell. Maynard then cut off Blackbeard's head, tied it by the hair to the ship's bowsprit, and returned triumphantly to Hampton Roads.

Tradition says that Blackbeard's head was placed on a pole at the mouth of the Hampton River at a place known afterward as Blackbeard's Point, to warn mariners against following his example. Someone is supposed to have taken the skull and made it into a huge drinking cup, which you might discover yourself in an antique shop, as it is believed to still be in existence.

The line is often vague between a pirate and a privateer. A pirate is generally known as one who robs at sea or plunders the land from the sea without commission from a sovereign nation. A privateer does the same thing, but is made respectable and legal by a commission from a government. A pirate is condemned, but a privateer is condoned, at least by his own government. Others tend to still think of him as a pirate.

The first instance of privateering on Chesapeake Bay was the action between Claiborne, representing Virginia, and Calvert, representing Maryland, in the dispute over which colony owned Kent Island.

Dutch privateers harassed English merchant ships in the Bay from 1662 to 1666. They captured thirteen ships and burned the HMS *Elizabeth* and five other ships off Newport News, Va.

While the French and English were at war on the continent in 1702, French privateers based in the West Indies preyed on English merchant ships in the Bay. They were also a menace in 1748.

During the Revolutionary War, the Americans called British sympathizers on Tangier Island picaroons. These men raided farms and estates and took ships as prizes all around the Bay. A patriot fleet based in Onancock, Va., in November of 1782 helped to deter them.

During the Revolutionary War and especially during the War of 1812, privateering provided an important offensive naval force for the struggling colonies. The fleet of 126 privateers took 556 British vessels during the War of 1812, or nearly one-third of the total taken by all American vessels, including the United States Navy.

Captain Thomas Boyle, a famous privateer captain during the War of 1812, conducted his successful ventures with great bravado.

He sent a dispatch to be posted in Lloyd's Coffee House in London, saying that by virtue of the power vested in him—that is, his commission and his schooner *Chasseur*, 356 tons, 150 men and 16 long 12-pound guns—he was blockading the entire coastline of the United Kingdom and Ireland.

Shipping losses to Baltimore privateers made the British vow to wipe out that "nest of pirates" on the Chesapeake.

On Sept. 12, 1814, British troops landed at North Point and marched on Baltimore. But their general was killed, and they were turned back. On Sept. 13, the British fleet bombarded Fort McHenry in the battle that inspired Francis Scott Key to compose "The Star-Spangled Banner."

The city of Baltimore still celebrates Sept. 12 as Defender's Day, in honor of the men killed defending Baltimore that day in 1814. Baltimore is the only major city on the East Coast never to have been captured by a foreign enemy.

Although the threat from pirates and privateers was largely over by then, construction of Fort Monroe was begun in 1819 at Old Point Comfort to protect the mouth of the Bay from such intruders.

Robert E. Lee helped to build the fort, and his quarters there are still occupied by a military family.

The fort finally achieved its fame, not as a protection against pirates, but as a Union stronghold during the Civil War, and as the place where Jefferson Davis, President of the Confederate States, was held prisoner.

Today Fort Monroe is the only moat-encircled fort in the United States still in active service.

Individuals and Deeds: An Alphabetical Assortment

Bacon's Rebellion was the first attempt in the New World to overthrow constituted authority by force.

Nathaniel Bacon, a member of the Virginia Council, wished to have a commission to proceed against an Indian rebellion in 1675. When Governor Berkeley refused, Bacon raised an army anyway and forced granting of the commission. Berkeley then fled to the Eastern Shore. Bacon assumed leadership of the government and sent a ship to capture the governor. Berkeley captured the ship instead and returned to Jamestown. Thereupon Bacon took the town by force and burned it. Bacon died while trying to gain supporters for his cause.

Commodore Joshua Barney, with a small flotilla of especially designed, shallow-draft barges, inflicted considerable damage on some larger English ships during the War of 1812 with hit-and-run tactics. Although the British subsequently marched on the nation's capital, Barney is credited with delaying the British attack on Washington by confronting the fleet on St. Leonard's Creek, a tributary of the Patuxent River.

Women's lib surfaced in Maryland way back in the seventeenth century when Mistress Margaret Brent became the first woman to claim the right of suffrage in America. Ms. Margaret Brent, as she would now be called, was born in England in 1600 and came to the new colony of Maryland in 1638 with a sister and two brothers. First settling in St. Mary's, the sisters brought letters which granted them the privilege of holding land just as the earliest settlers had done. When the grant was recorded, Margaret Brent became the first woman to hold land in her own right in Maryland.

After Governor Leonard Calvert's death in 1647, she became executrix of his estate and guardian of his children. But when she asked for two votes in the Assembly—one because she owned land, and one because she was attorney for the late Leonard Calvert—the new governor refused to grant her request.

Seven Calverts influenced the history of Maryland. Six of them held the title of Lord Baltimore.

Joshua Barney forces the British to retreat

George Calvert was the first Lord Baltimore. King James I promised to give him a charter to settle the territory which became Maryland. But before the charter was actually granted in 1632, George died, and the charter was given to his son, Cecilius, second Lord Baltimore and first proprietor of Maryland.

Leonard Calvert was governor of Maryland, but not a Lord Baltimore. He was the brother of Cecilius Calvert, second Lord Baltimore. He came to the new colony with the first settlers on the *Ark* and the *Dove* in 1634.

Charles Calvert, son of Cecilius, was the third Lord Baltimore, and his son, Benedict Leonard Calvert, was the fourth Lord Baltimore. Benedict died only six weeks after his father, so his son, Charles, quickly succeeded to his position as fifth Lord Baltimore.

Charles' son, Frederick Calvert, was the sixth and last Lord Baltimore. It was he, along with descendants of William Penn, who finally settled the long boundary quarrel between Maryland and Pennsylvania by accepting the Mason and Dixon Line as the border.

———

Patty Cannon was known as the first lady of crime of Maryland and Delaware during her life, which ended violently in 1829. Patty earned her infamous title while living near the Nanticoke River at Johnson's Crossroads, which straddled the two state lines. There she kidnapped free negroes to sell into slavery and also stole slaves for resale in the deep South.

She gained a reputation as a murderer, and is said to have killed her husband. Patty died of poison in the jail at Georgetown, Del. Because of her gangster-like life, the name Patty Cannon was used to scare naughty children in those days.

———

Scarcely known today, Miss Anna Ella Carroll gained fame in Civil War times as an unofficial public relations counsel to President Lincoln and as a military strategist. Her grave is at Old Trinity Church, on Church Creek, near Cambridge.

It was her plan to send gunboats up the Tennessee River, wipe out forts there and split the South in half all the way to Mobile Bay.

———

William Claiborne, a colonist of some prominence in early Virginia, settled and built a fort on Kent Island in 1631 for the purpose of trading with the Indians. In 1634, Lord Baltimore claimed that Kent Island belonged to Maryland under his charter from the king, while Claiborne still claimed it for Virginia. Armed battle and pressure from the company Claiborne traded with in England gave Lord Baltimore and Maryland control. When King Charles was beheaded in England and the royal governor of Maryland was removed, then Claiborne and Virginia were back in power. Lord Baltimore later succeeded in having his claim reinstated and fighting broke out again. In 1658, a treaty gave Kent Island to Maryland and ended Claiborne's claim forever.

———

John Custis I emigrated to the colonies about 1640. His son, John

Custis II, built a house on Virginia's Eastern Shore where Governor William Berkeley took refuge during Bacon's Rebellion in 1676. John Custis IV inherited this estate, named Arlington, on Old Plantation Creek, and it was here he brought his bride, Frances Parke.

John and Frances had a son, Daniel Parke Custis, who married Martha Dandridge. When Martha was widowed, she married George Washington.

But before Daniel died, Martha and Daniel had a son, John Custis V, who inherited land on the Potomac River, which he called Arlington after his grandfather's estate on Old Plantation Creek. Robert E. Lee acquired this Arlington by marrying into the Custis family. The estate was confiscated during the Civil War and is now our National Cemetery.

Besides being members of these old and prestigious and intertwined families, John Custis IV and Frances are best remembered because they did not get along well together and frequently spoke to each other by relaying messages through the butler. Once John invited Frances to go for a drive and drove their buggy into Old Plantation Creek. Frances finally asked where they were going. He answered, "Hell, Madam." John gave the same reply when Frances repeated the question as the horse began to swim. Then Frances said, "Drive on. I am not afraid to go where you will go. The Devil will be cheated of his own until he gets you."

"The Devil, Hell and nothing else will scare you, so I had as well return," was all John could think of to say, and he drove out of the creek.

They continued to live together many years until Frances died, seven years before John. By John's own direction, the following is included in his epitaph.

"Aged 71 years and yet lived but 7 years which was the space of time he kept A Bachelor's House at Arlington On the Eastern Shore of Virginia."

Legend says that John Custis IV was buried standing up, but does not explain why.

———

Frederick Douglass, whose real name was Frederick Augustus Bailey, began life as a slave in Talbot County in 1817. He struggled to educate himself and wrote "Narrative of the Life of Frederick Douglass," published in 1845 after he had escaped from slavery. He became influential in Washington and was Minister to Haiti at one time. One of his homes, near the Capitol in Washington, D.C., is now a museum of African Art. Another, across the Anacostia River from Washington, D.C., is owned by the National Park Service and is open to the public.

———

If Thomas, sixth Lord Fairfax, could be brought back to life, he

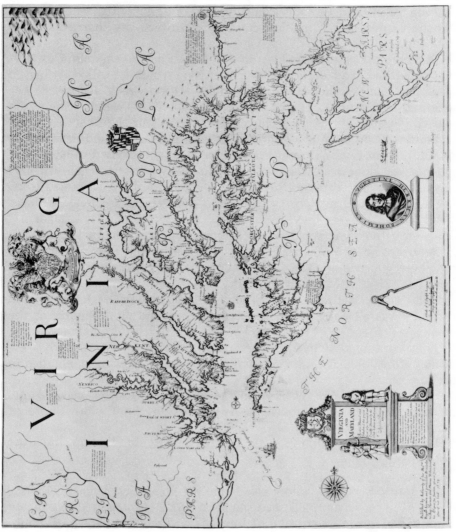

Augustine Herrman's important map of Chesapeake Bay, 1670. U.S. Library of Congress

probably would not survive the sight of the beltways, suburbs, condominiums and shopping centers covering northern Virginia. He once was proprietor of all that land.

To be specific, his land included all that "bounded within the heads of the rivers Rappahannock and Potomac," or the 5,200,000 acres of the present counties of Lancaster, Northumberland, Richmond, Westmoreland, Warren, Stafford, King George, Prince William, Fairfax, Loudoun, Fauquier, Rappahannock, Culpeper, Clarke, Madison, Page, Shenandoah, and Frederick in Virginia, and Hardy, Hampshire, Morgan, Berkeley, and Jefferson in West Virginia.

John Frazier, provost marshal of Kent County, Md., wanted to become clerk of the court in 1860. So he declared a state of emergency, which brought two government transports filled with soldiers from Baltimore to Chestertown, the county seat. He arrested the rival candidates and their chief supporters and sent them to Baltimore on the transports. Then he stationed the troops at the polls to be sure he and his party would win the election.

Justice eventually prevailed, and Frazier was arrested and sent to Baltimore to face charges himself.

Lillie Mae Capel Flowers became the first woman anywhere in the United States to be licensed to operate commercial power vessels on the bays, rivers and oceans, when she became a commercial captain on Chesapeake Bay in 1937.

In 1940, Captain D'Arcy Grant, skipper of the schooner *Fannie Insley*, was the only female skipper of a sailing vessel engaged in hauling freight on the Chesapeake.

John Hanson, in 1781, was the first president of the United States under the Articles of Confederation, preceding George Washington in office by eight years. He was born in Mulberry Grove, near Port Tobacco, on the Potomac River, in 1721 and died in 1783. He is the only Marylander to have served as president of the United States.

To help settle disputes over the boundaries of his land, Lord Baltimore commissioned Augustine Herrman to draw a map of Maryland and Virginia. Herrman drew one which was considered authentic for the next 200 years, and which he entitled "Virginia and Maryland As it is Planted and Inhabited this present Year 1670 Surveyed and Exactly Drawne by the Only Labour and Endeavor of Augustine Herrman Bohemiensis."

In return for the map and for some other surveying tasks, the grateful Lord Baltimore gave Herrman a grant of between 20,000 and 25,000 acres in 1671, between the Bohemia and Elk Rivers, and made him the first naturalized citizen of the New World.

Francis Scott Key wrote "The Star-Spangled Banner" while detained on a British ship during the bombardment of Fort McHenry in 1814. The earliest known manuscript of our national anthem is on exhibit at the Maryland Historical Society in Baltimore.

Fort McHenry's flag, which inspired Key, was the largest United States battle flag ever flown. It measured 30 feet by 42 feet overall.

Flag House — Baltimore

Each stripe was 24 inches wide, and each of the 15 five-pointed stars was 24 inches from point to point. It was handmade by Mary Young Pickersgill in her home in Baltimore, known today as the Flag House. The flag hangs in the Smithsonian Institution.

Kitty Knight became famous when the English forces under Admiral Cockburn burned Georgetown on the Sassafras River during the War of 1812. The young and beautiful Kitty is supposed to have beaten out the flames consuming her home with a broom and spoken sharply to the soldiers, thus saving her home. The house still stands and has been converted to an attractive restaurant.

Francis Makemie was the founder of the Presbyterian Church in America. In 1705-1706 he built the Rehobeth Presbyterian Church, near Princess Anne, Md., now the oldest organized Presbyterian Church and congregation in America. Makemie Park, five miles from Temperanceville, on Holden's Creek, is dedicated to this early churchman and a stone monument honors him in Onancock.

Thurgood Marshall, who was born in Baltimore, was the first black to be appointed to the United States Supreme Court in 1967.

He had been refused admission to the University of Maryland Law School, so he studied law at Howard University, where he graduated at the top of his class. Marshall was responsible in 1935 for getting the first black admitted to the University of Maryland Law School by proving that the state had no equal facility for blacks.

Charles Mason and Jeremiah Dixon were surveyors hired to settle a dispute between William Penn and Lord Baltimore over the boundaries of Maryland and Pennsylvania, in 1763. The contention was over who owned the land between the thirty-ninth and fortieth parallels of latitude.

When King Charles II gave William Penn a charter in 1681, the southern boundary was the beginning of the fortieth parallel of latitude. Penn's charter did not include any part of the Bay, as he had hoped it would. So Penn decided to interpret the beginning of the fortieth parallel as the thirty-ninth parallel, which passes near the present site of Baltimore. Lord Baltimore disagreed.

The feud raged until Lord Baltimore and Penn mutually petitioned the king to settle the matter. A temporary line was established in 1738. In 1763, Mason and Dixon were chosen to survey a new line, which they ran west for 162 miles before the Indians said that was far enough.

The Middle Point stone marker between Maryland and Delaware placed by Mason and Dixon still stands beneath a brick pavilion surrounded by a low iron fence on Route 455 north and west of Salisbury.

Beside it are two other stones. One marks the end of the Transpeninsular Line, already there when Mason and Dixon surveyed. No one seems to know what the other stone marks, so it is left there in case it is important.

Stones marking the lines surveyed by Mason and Dixon were placed one mile apart, with an M on the Maryland side, a P on the Pennsylvania side, and a D on the Delaware side.

Matthew Fontaine Maury was born in Virginia, in 1806. He became a midshipman in the Navy. A stagecoach accident which crippled his leg kept him from sea duty, so he served as Superintendent of the Naval Observatory and Hydrographic Office from 1841 to 1861. He studied winds and current and charted the Atlantic, Pacific, and Indian Oceans. He was the first to describe the Gulf Stream.

One of his biographers said, "No single individual has done more for his fellow man in lessening the hazards of navigation than Matthew Fontaine Maury."

———

Robert Morris, Sr., came to Oxford in 1738 and established himself as the agent for Foster, Cunliffe, Esq., of Liverpool. As the storekeeper he was a leading citizen of the town. His son, also named Robert Morris, became known as the Financier of the American Revolution, was the first United States Superintendent of Finance, and a member of Congress.

Robert Morris, Sr., came to an untimely end when the wadding from a gun which was being fired in salute as he left a moored merchant ship hit him in the elbow. The wound festered and he died.

———

William Paca, of Annapolis and Wye Island, was one of the few men who both signed and voted for the Declaration of Independence in 1776. He acquired a large sum of money by marrying into the Lloyd family and built Wye Hall, described as the grandest house on the Eastern Shore, at a cost of 20,000 pounds sterling. Carvel Hall, now being restored, was his Annapolis residence.

———

Sir Peter Parker became famous in American history for his attack on the Eastern Shore which diverted attention from the attack on Baltimore by the English in 1814. Parker and his British forces landed near Tolchester (later to become a popular summer beach resort) with 260 men. He met Col. Philip Reed and his Americans on Caulk's Field on Aug. 31, 1814, and was defeated and killed. A stone monument stands on the site, dedicated to the patriotism and fortitude of both the victor and the vanquished.

This was the first land victory for the Americans within the Chesapeake area and a prelude to the victory in Baltimore.

———

Charles Willson Peale, the famous artist who founded the Maryland State Museum of Natural History and was influential in establishing the Academy of Fine Arts, was born in Chestertown, Md., in 1741.

———

John Rablie, of Virginia, was the first pilot on Bay waters. Virginia first licensed pilots in 1661. They were charged with keeping beacons in repair as well as with guiding ships. Today pilots board boats entering the Bay just inside Cape Henry. The run up the Bay is said to be the second longest pilotage in the world.

Thomas Savage came to Virginia in 1607, when he was only 13 years old. Captain Newport gave him to the Indian chief, Powhatan, in exchange for an Indian named Namotacke, and Savage lived with Powhatan for several years. He went to the Eastern Shore in 1619 and Debedeavon, the Indian leader there, gave him 9,000 acres of land known thereafter as Savage's Neck, between Cheriton Creek and King's Creek.

Thomas Savage is the first of the Jamestown arrivals whose descendants are known. If your name is Savage, you have the oldest name in the United States.

Two young tourists visit the marker commemorating the Battle of Caulk's Field, the Americans' first victory in the Chesapeake area in the War of 1812. Anne M. Hays

Grace Sherwood lived near Virginia Beach. In 1706, she was accused of witchcraft. She was taken to a pond called Witch Duck, bound and thrown in the water by the sheriff. By some means she got ashore and managed to live 34 years longer.

How she avoided the fate of most witches is not recorded. Usually witches were considered guilty if they floated, so they were hanged. They were considered innocent only if they sank!

Joshua Thomas is the best known early proponent of Methodism in the Bay area. Known as "The Parson of the Islands," he traveled in a log canoe called *The Methodist.* He is remembered for preaching to the 12,000 British troops who assembled on Tangier Island in 1814, prior

Joshua Thomas — at Tangier Island

to their attack on Baltimore. He correctly and courageously predicted during the service that the British attack (during which Francis Scott Key wrote "The Star-Spangled Banner") would be unsuccessful.

Thomas died in 1853, at the age of 77, and is buried on Deal Island.

Tench Tilghman, a member of a prominent Bay area family, was a military aide to General George Washington. It was Tench Tilghman who carried the news of Cornwallis' surrender at Yorktown in 1781 to Philadelphia, where the new American government was headquartered.

Tench Tilghman

Tilghman traveled from York Harbor, Va., to Annapolis, Md., by open boat, and from Annapolis to Rock Hall, Md., by another boat, losing some hours when the boat went aground. He rode from Rock Hall to Philadelphia in two days, a trip which now requires only two hours by car. He called for fresh horses along the way by shouting, "Cornwallis is taken. A fresh horse for the Congress."

Harriet Tubman, a black woman born a slave in 1820 at Bucktown, Md., (near Cambridge), gained fame for guiding more than 300 slaves from the Eastern Shore to Canada after she ran away from her master. During the Civil War, she was commissioned by Union leaders as a spy and scout. In ten years, she made 19 trips to Canada, and none of the slaves she guided was ever caught.

She was praised by the United States Secretary of State, William Seward; sent a medal by Queen Victoria; and given a medal by Congress.

She is commemorated by a monument in Auburn, N.Y., where she died in 1913, and by a bronze tablet placed near her Bucktown birthplace.

Harriet Tubman leading escaped slaves

Mason Locke Weems, also known as Parson Weems, was a Virginian who became famous as the author of biographies of American national heroes. It was he who wrote the biography of George Washington around 1800, which contained for the first time the stories of chopping down the cherry tree and throwing the dollar across the Rappahannock River. Some scholars feel that Parson Weems may have taken a few liberties with facts.

Lambert Wickes was born about 1742, on Eastern Neck Island, now a national wildlife refuge. He became a sea captain and was placed in command of the warship *Reprisal* during the Revolutionary War. He captured a number of prizes on a voyage to the French West Indies. In recognition of his ability, the Congress appointed him to carry Benjamin Franklin (American Minister to France at the time) to Paris. After safely delivering Franklin, Wickes distinguished himself by severely harassing English shipping. He and his ship were finally lost in September 1777. Because many of his personal papers and records went down with him, his exploits were virtually unknown in the United States until French and English archives were researched.

A mysterious female stranger lies beneath an elaborate marble monument in St. Paul's Cemetery in Alexandria, Va. According to a romantic story handed down by word of mouth, a lady and her male companion disembarked from a ship in Alexandria harbor in 1816. The lady was ill, and although cared for by a doctor and nurse at Gadsby's Tavern, she soon died. Her companion disappeared. Rumor gave them many names, but none were ever confirmed.

How They Amused Themselves

Long before the first colonists arrived, the Bay Indians liked to gather at certain times of the year on the shores of the Bay's tributaries to eat oysters. This old Indian custom is still observed by many Bay residents today.

Every year when the Indians gathered to eat oysters, they added more shells to the pile of empties from the previous year. These piles of empty oystershells are known as midden heaps.

The biggest and oldest oystershell midden heap on record is said to have been 18 to 20 feet deep and to have covered 30 acres of land near Popes Creek, on the Potomac River.

Sometimes the Indians included roast potatoes on the menu for their oyster feasts. The first recorded mention of this by a colonist was made by John Pory, the Secretary of the Virginia Colony, in 1621, when he was the guest of Ekees, the King of the Onancocks. John Pory, the story goes, burned his mouth on a hot potato and said later, "I would not give a farthing for a shipload."

The English settlers imported their native sport of foxhunting to the New World. Robert Brooke, of Queen Annes County, Md., was the first to hunt fox in the colonies, probably as early as 1650.

Local grey fox were hunted until red fox were imported from England. The arrival of the red fox in Chestertown, Md., was celebrated with a grand ball.

Franklin Weems, owner of Mount Republican, an estate built in 1792 between Popes Creek and Cedar Point on the Potomac River, loved foxhunting so much that he kept a pack of 100 foxhounds. He was most famous, however, for his love of parties, and he gave them three

Fox hunting is still a popular sport in Maryland. Maryland Department of Economic and Community Development

times a week, earning for himself the title of "King Entertainer of Southern Maryland." He also had a continuous poker game in session at his home for 40 years, said to be the longest continuous poker game on record. Unfortunately, the reason for the game finally concluding is not known.

The South River Club, said to be the oldest social organization with a continuous history in the entire United States, is tangible proof that the colonists liked to get together for fun and good food.

The club originally met for dinner every two weeks, but now meets less frequently.

The club still meets in its clubhouse which dates from 1742. The original one burned in 1741. It is located between Glebe Creek on the South River and the West River. Look for the historical marker describing it on Route 2, south of Annapolis.

Early in Virginia's colonial history, it was against the law to give a theatrical performance. However, three men performed in a play called "Ye Beare and Ye Cubb" in Pungoteague, on the Eastern Shore of Virginia, Aug. 27, 1665. This is believed to have been the first play staged in the New World.

The three men were charged with "acting a play," but were found not guilty, in spite of the fact that the court hearing the case inspected the costumes and script.

The first theater in America was built in Williamsburg, in 1718. Both professional and amateur productions were staged there. Because of financial difficulties, the playhouse was given to the city for a town hall in 1745. In 1751, a second theater was built in Williamsburg.

Annapolis was the second town in America to have a theater. One was built there in 1752. By that year, traveling companies were touring Bayside towns like Chestertown, Baltimore, Annapolis, and Upper Marlboro, presenting plays with titles like "The Lone Trapper."

Chesapeake Bay had its own showboat, *The James Adams Floating Theater*, for 25 years during the early 1900's.

From its winter berth in North Carolina, the boat traveled from town to town around Chesapeake Bay, beginning in early March and returning south to escape the winter ice.

The actors and actresses, Mrs. Adams and Mr. Adams' sister and her husband, performed in a different play each night the boat was docked in a town. Seats cost 50 cents or less, and about 500 people could be seated for one performance.

The showboat was built in 1914, measured about 130 feet in length, about 35 feet in width and, unloaded, required only 15 inches of water to float in. Two gasoline towboats, *The Elk* and *The Trouper*, towed her around the Bay.

The James Adams Floating Theater gained particular fame when Edna Ferber's novel, "Showboat," became popular. In preparation for writing the novel, Miss Ferber had done some of her research aboard the Adams floating theater. When a movie was made of the novel, James Adams took advantage of the reflected glory by painting "The Original Floating Theater" in three-foot letters on his boat, even though it was not the original floating theater.

The boat was sold by the Adamses to Mrs. Nina S. Howard around 1930, when talking pictures began to compete with it and deplete the profits. The showboat tied up in Baltimore to give performances in December 1939, for the last time. She burned in the Savannah River, on Nov. 14, 1941.

―――――

Prizefighting, like play-acting, is a form of entertainment, now legal, which was once tantalizingly outside the law.

On Feb. 2, 1849, an illegal bout for the heavyweight championship title of the United States took place on a farm bordering Worton Creek, in Kent County, Md., where the combatants and spectators had fled to escape from the pursuing police.

The fighters were Tom Hyer, the generally recognized champion, and Yankee Sullivan, the contender, fresh from an undefeated foreign tour.

The fight was scheduled to take place on Poole's Island, which was deserted at that time except for two run-down buildings where the fighters and their followers spent the night before the fight.

The police arrived at Poole's Island by boat from Baltimore in the morning, but did not succeed in arresting either fighter. They stormed upstairs in one building and arrested Hyer's trainer, while Hyer himself slipped out a window and onto a boat. Then they confronted Sullivan and his sparring partner in the second building. Sullivan thought fast, pushed his companion and shouted, "Run, Sullivan!" The police made chase after the wrong man, and Sullivan was left alone to wade offshore to a waiting boat.

The fighters, their friends, and some of the spectators sailed over to Worton Creek to Mr. W.A. Gibson's farm and proceeded with the fight. Hyer won in either 15 or 16 rounds and received the purse of $10,000.

The police finally did catch up with Hyer, however, and he was fined $1,000 for his part in the fight.

―――――

Hunting wildfowl for food and sport has always been a popular form of recreation in the Bay Country, and the source of many good stories.

One is that "Cook" Webster went duck hunting one day in the boat that he and Will Northram owned jointly—the first gasoline-powered boat in Solomons, in 1901.

When the engine refused to start after the day's shooting, the frustrated Webster shot a hole through the engine and through the bottom of the boat, which promptly sank. The boat's name was *Naughty*.

———

Most hunters enjoy the aid and companionship of a good hunting dog, and the Chesapeake Bay Retriever is a popular breed in the Bay Country.

The Chesapeake Bay Retriever is one of only four breeds of dog native to the United States, and it is the only sporting breed native to the United States.

Some say it is the result of breeding a female Irish setter with a male otter. More likely the breed comes from the mating of local retrievers with the male and female Newfoundland puppies rescued from a sinking ship in 1807.

The dog has a dense undercoat which protects it from severe weather, and a reddish-tan outercoat which blends well with marshy cover.

One noted Chesapeake Bay Retriever, named "Old Sailor," was said to have retrieved 100 wildfowl in a single day of hunting.

The Chesapeake Bay Retriever was named the official state dog of Maryland in 1964.

Marriage Oaks

When the line dividing Maryland and Virginia on the Eastern Shore was surveyed in 1663, several large oak trees were selected as boundary monuments. Because it was easier to get married in Maryland than in Virginia, it became fairly common for Virginia couples to cross the line and be wed in the shade of these trees on the north side. Consequently, they became known as marriage oaks.

Boats have been an important part of Bay Country social life since the first colonists arrived. Boats were primarily used for commercial transportation of people and goods, but they were used occasionally by their owners for pleasure and to make social visits. The first yacht used solely for pleasure did not appear on the Bay until 1689. She was the *Susanna*, owned by Major Richard Sewale.

In 1774, boatowners were betting on the outcome of boat races held on the Potomac and Rappahannock Rivers.

An early account of such races follows:

"The Boats were to Start, to use the Language of Jockeys, immediately after Dinner; A Boat was anchored down the River at a Mile Distance—Captain Dobby and Captain Benson steer'd the Boats in the Race—Captain Benson had 5 Oarsmen; Captain Dobby had 6—It was Ebb Tide—The Betts were small and chiefly given to the Negroes who rowed—Captain Benson won the first Race—Captain Purchace offered to bett ten Dollars that with the same Boat and same Hands, only having Liberty to put a small Weight in the Stern, he would beat Captain Benson—He was taken and came out best only half the Boats Length."

The first recorded sailing regattas on Chesapeake Bay were held in 1760.

Now sailboats race almost every summer weekend, and sometimes in the fall, winter and spring too, in all parts of the Bay, competing not for high stakes, but for fun, prestige and trophies.

Powerboat racing takes several forms, with predicted log and navigators' contests probably attracting the greatest participation. At various ports around the Bay, groups hold competitions several times during the boating season, culminating in one large gathering for each district each summer.

Recently several local squadrons of the U.S. Power Squadron have conducted predicted log contests for trailerable powerboats in addition to competition for inboard cruisers.

Speedboats and small hydroplanes also hold racing meets at various Bay locations.

IV. IN, OVER AND AROUND CHESAPEAKE BAY

Shellfish

Oysters

The colonists first tasted Bay oysters in 1607 on Cape Henry, when they happened upon a group of Indians who were roasting some. The Indians were frightened and ran away. The colonists stayed to eat the oysters and described them as large and delicious.

In 1610, a man named Strachey wrote that he had seen an oyster 13 inches long. Another colonist bragged that Bay oysters were four times as big as English oysters.

In 1607, colonists found oysters and mussels lying on the ground as thick as stones at Lynnhaven Bay. They also reported finding pearls inside some of the oysters. But the round objects found in Bay oysters are chalky, dull and valueless, though they are formed around an irritating particle or infection in the same way as pearls are. About one in every 10,000 Bay oysters will contain one of these round objects.

The custom of not eating oysters during months without an R in their name (May—August) developed because oysters spoil quickly during the summer months if refrigeration is not available and they reproduce during those months. (Oysters are actually in their poorest condition for eating during September, an R month, because their energy has been depleted by reproduction.)

Hand tonging oysters

A pink oyster is something like a purple cow—startling, but harmless. The pink color is caused by a pigment in something the oyster has eaten which does not affect either the wholesomeness or taste of the oyster. The color may develop anytime up to five days after packing and disappears with the heat of cooking.

An oyster with a green gill will not make you feel a bit green about the gills yourself if you eat it. The green color is caused by a simple plant organism the oyster has eaten which gives the oyster an especially good flavor.

An oyster would appear to be well protected by its thick shell. But one of his natural enemies, a snail called an oyster drill, has a long

Patent tonging oyster boats crowd into Annapolis Harbor. Maryland Department of Economic and Community Development

tongue like a file which can rasp a small hole right into the shell. Then the oyster drill inserts its flexible snout and eats the oyster without opening the shell.

Diseases, such as MSX and Dermocystidium, are also devastating to oysters. Scientists are trying to develop oysters which are resistant to these diseases, and which are also fast growing and of desirable shape.

In so doing they have developed oysters which reach the three-inch market size in 18 months, instead of the normal 30-months' growing time.

———

In 1972, the first Annual Chesapeake Bay Oyster Shucking Championship was held at the St. Mary's Oyster Festival. Ron Evans, who shucked a dozen oysters in 55 seconds flat, won the title, and his record was not bettered in either the 1973 or 1974 contest.

The oyster wars of the late 1800's were caused by illegal oyster dredgers stealing oysters from beds worked by legal oyster tongers. During the 30 years the wars lasted, about 50 men were killed, including watermen and policemen from the Maryland Oyster Navy, commissioned in 1868.

More trouble erupted in the 1940's and 1950's, this time over who should control the Potomac River oyster beds. The dispute between Maryland and Virginia watermen was sometimes carried out with

An oyster buy boat waits to collect the day's catch from the oystermen when they return to Annapolis Harbor. Anne M. Hays

machine guns and was finally settled by an agreement between state officials.

A Maryland law, enacted in 1894, gave special permission "to any woman who has no visible means of support to take and catch oysters without a license." The phrase "no visible means of support" was later deleted, thereby allowing any woman to take oysters in Maryland without a license.

In 1973, when Maryland legislators deleted discriminatory references to women, the first three words in the law reading "No woman and no person more than 64 years of age shall be required to pay the license

Crab house at Smith Island. Maryland Department of Economic and Community Development

fee specified" were removed. Now a female oysterman less than 64 years of age must buy a license to take oysters legally in Maryland.

Also in 1973, Maryland legally allowed diving for oysters for the first time, with the same catch limit as for tongers.

Virginia owns about 210,000 acres of submerged land which are public oyster grounds. Another 134,000 acres of submerged, state-owned lands which do not naturally produce oysters are rented to citizens for private production.

Maryland's shellfish hatchery at Horn's Point expects to be able to produce 500 or 600 million oysters and 200 million hard clams of plantable size yearly to replenish and supplement the natural reproduction of these shellfish.

An oyster of three inches or larger, in water 50° F. or warmer, will pump approximately 50 gallons of water daily through itself to obtain food and oxygen, according to the Maryland Department of Natural Resources. Other sources state figures from 25 to 144 gallons as their estimate of how much water an oyster can pump through itself in a 24-hour period. Because oysters are extracting proteins, carbohydrates, fats, salts and minerals from the water as it passes through, scientists at Wood's Hole, in Massachusetts, are experimenting with using oysters as a final stage sewage treatment plant, and are able to eat the oysters when they grow fat!

Experiments have shown that oysters in a hatchery which receives warmer than normal water from power plant cooling towers grow more uniformly and to a higher quality in significantly less time than oysters grown in ordinary Bay water.

The Swan Point Bar, off Rock Hall, Md., is considered by many to be the largest natural oyster bed in the world.

A Dorchester County superstition says it is a good thing to sing while you are catching oysters.

Buried oyster reefs are sometimes mined for their oystershells. These shells are used as cultch (material to which young oysters may attach themselves and grow), for shell lime, filler for wallboard, ballast for stabilizing roadbeds, and as chicken feed.

Crabs

Before steaming turns them brilliant orange-red, blue crabs really are blue, especially on their claws. They are equipped with five pairs of legs. The front pair are claws that pinch wickedly if you have the misfortune to meet a defensive crab. These claws also are their means of feeding. The back legs are called swimmerettes and propel the crab through the water. The middle three pairs are used for walking.

To talk about the life cycle of a blue crab, you must know the language. Here's how to "talk crab" like an expert.

Adult female crabs, or sooks, migrate in October and November, or in May, to the area of the Virginia Capes to lay eggs. Each sook lays an average of one and one-half million eggs, of which only about one ten-thousandth of one percent of those laid needs to hatch and grow to maturity to replace the population. While carrying the eggs, the female crab is called a sponge, or berry crab, or busted sook.

Crab megalops

MH

The eggs develop through two larval stages, the zoeal and the megalopine, and eventually become crabs. Occasionally in late August or early September, large numbers of megalops appear in the surf off Virginia Beach and bite swimmers with their minute pinching claws. Uneducated swimmers complain of water fleas, but you will know they are megalops.

A crab sheds an average of 18 or 20 times to reach its maximum growth.

When a crab cracks its old shell just before shedding, it is called a buster. Without the old shell, the crustacean is classified as a soft crab. During the approximately two hours it takes for the new shell to begin to harden, the crab expands by absorbing moisture, increasing its size by one-quarter to one-third. Experts say the difference in the size of mature crabs is due to different percentage increases in size at each moult. The percentage varies according to genetic and environmental factors. Water absorption may be greater, for example, when the salinity level of the water is low.

A crab caught by Phil Barr in the 1968 National Hard Crab Derby fishing contest, which measured 14 inches across, may be the largest ever caught in the Bay.

A crab is a papershell for 9 to 12 hours after shedding because the new shell as it forms is papery, or leathery, in texture.

Before the shell becomes hard, it is stiff and brittle for 12 to 24 hours. In this stage, a crab is called a buckram. A peeler is a hard crab with a fully-formed soft shell beneath the hard one, ready to start the whole process of moulting all over again.

An adult male crab is called a jimmy, a jimmy-dick, or a channeler, because it is sometimes found in the deep river channels. When mating, the male crab cradle-carries a mature female for two or three days, to protect her when she has shed her shell, and the two crabs are called a doubler.

Amateur crabbers usually catch crabs with a handline, a dip net or by skimming from a moving boat. Professional crabbers usually catch crabs with crab pots or trotlines.

A crab pot is an intricate device which entices crabs to come in after the bait, then will not let them out. You will find crab pots attached by a line to the floats which dot the shallow areas of the Bay. (To tamper with or disturb these crab pots is illegal, though.) Crab pots were invented and patented by B.F. Lewis, of Harryhogan, Va., around 1938.

Trotlining is an adaptation of the old English practice of longlining. Watermen of Chesapeake Bay tie a piece of bait every 10 feet on a long length of line. After the line is anchored at one end, it is unwound to await the hungry crabs. When the line is rewound, feeding crabs are scooped up with a net.

Watermen say that hard crabs have more meat in them when the moon is on the wane, and that soft crabs are best and most plentiful when the moon is full.

A female crab lives two years and a male crab lives three. A blue crab eats decaying fish or meat, and marine vegetation. Jellyfish, comb jellies and fish are a crab's enemies.

Crabbing as an industry began about 1873, when a shipment of soft crabs was sent from Crisfield, Md., to Philadelphia. The harvest of hard

Soft-shell clams, or maninose, are harvested with this rig which shoots the clams onto the conveyor belt hydraulically. Maryland Department of Economic and Community Development

crabs that year amounted to a little over three million pounds taken in Virginia and Maryland waters. Since it takes 1.75 crabs to equal one pound of crabs, three million pounds represented between five and six million crabs.

By 1915, this had risen to 50,400,000 pounds, but in 1920 had dropped back to 22,700,000 pounds, due to lack of conservation, in the opinion of some observers.

Chesapeake Bay crabs constitute about two-thirds of the entire United States' blue crab harvest. In 1973, 33,156,730 pounds of blue crabs were harvested from Chesapeake Bay and its tributaries.

Researchers would like to brand crabs to help them study crab population and movements. But how do you brand something like a crab, that sheds its shell frequently? Branding with a laser beam, which alters some of the pigmentation cells under the outer shell, may be the answer, as new outer shells will also carry such a brand. Freeze branding, using a copper branding iron cooled to subzero temperatures to alter the pigmentation cells, is being used experimentally in Oregon.

Tagging with small plastic tags is another way of marking crabs so they are recognizable. A crab-tagging program conducted by the Chesapeake Biological Laboratory has shown that crabs can travel amazing distances. When released along the Chesapeake and Delaware Canal at the head of Chesapeake Bay, some of the crabs moved east into the Delaware River while others moved into the Chesapeake. Best travel time averaged nearly four miles a day to a total of 97 miles in 27 days. Another record crab swim was a 55-day jaunt down to Tilghman Island, a distance of 84 miles.

The study was undertaken to determine the extent that blue crabs migrate between Chesapeake and Delaware Bays and to determine the effect of enlarging the canal.

Clams

Hard-shell clams may be found from the high-water mark to about the 60-foot depth, wherever the water is sufficiently salty (more than 15 parts of salt per one thousand parts of water).

The heaviest concentrations of hard-shell clams in the Bay are found on the north side of the lower York River and the Coleman Bridge vicinity; the Tue Marsh-Back Creek area; Poquoson Flats; the southern section of the Willoughby-Crumps Banks area; Hampton Flats; and the lower James River.

Cherrystone Inlet is located on the Bay side of Virginia's Eastern Shore, north of Cape Charles. But Cherrystone clams do not necessarily come from that inlet. Cherrystone is a trade name denoting the size of the clam.

Cherrystone clams need two to eight years to reach marketable size. Larger chowder clams require eight to twenty years to develop, according to the National Marine Fisheries Service. The clam's growth rate is slower and the mortality rate is higher during years when unusually high rainfall lowers the salinity of the Bay water.

Clams in salty areas, like Hampton Flats, grow faster than clams in the less salty lower York River.

The legal size for keeping hard-shell clams is one inch across the thickest part of the hinge.

A hard-shell clam is either male or female at any time, but it can change its sex from one year to another.

The coastal Indians made wampum from the purple part of this clam's shell.

———

Chesapeake Bay soft-shell clams are known as maninose. The clams dig down into the soft sandy Bay bottom, leaving a tunnel for water to circulate to them, bringing food and oxygen.

Maninose clams were usually harvested in the Bay only for bait until 1952, when the clam beds in New England failed, opening up the New England consumer market to Bay clams. Soft-shell clam production in Chesapeake Bay increased ten times in the two years from 1954 to 1956, as Bay area people learned to eat clams too.

Soft-shell clams are usually harvested by washing the clams from the bottom with a hydraulic dredge. They are brought to the surface on an endless belt attached to the side of the boat.

Spawning occurs twice yearly in the Chesapeake, during May-June and September-October. Growth varies according to water currents, food supply, water temperature, and nature of the sediment. Under favorable conditions, a clam can grow to two inches in two years, or it may never grow that big in unfavorable conditions. Predators are bottom-feeding fish, ducks, swans and cow-nosed rays.

Finfish

An eighteenth century visitor to Chesapeake Bay wrote home that the fish were so plentiful they were obliged to swim on their sides.

The fish, while not that plentiful now, still attract thousands of sport fishermen and support large commercial fin and shellfish industries, which together produce 65 million dollars annually in revenue.

Two-hundred and thirty-eight recorded species of fish swim in the Bay and its tributaries. More than 32 of these species are caught commercially. Among the most common finfish in the Bay are herring, shad, trout, suckers, minnows, carp, catfish, crappies, perch, drum, rock and black bass.

Both Virginia and Maryland hold annual fishing tournaments, and record fish have been established for several species. A few of the outstanding records follow.

A Virginia woman, Betty D. Hall, holds the world record with the 111-pound black drum she caught at Cape Charles, Va. Mrs. Leroy Shipp caught a Bay-record 9-pound, 8-ounce speckled trout in the Corrotoman River near Weems, Va., in 1972. Some Bay-record fish caught in fly-fishing competitions are a 65-pound channel bass caught in 1970 in Tangier Sound; a striped bass (or rockfish), 50 pounds, one ounce, caught in 1965; and a cobia, 97 pounds, 12 ounces, caught in 1969.

Perhaps colonists' accounts of such monsters as shad a yard long and a 12-foot sturgeon are to be believed, after all.

Although most sport fishermen use a rod and reel to cast or troll while chumming or drifting in their pursuit of finfish, it is also lawful on the Bay at certain times of the year to spear fish or shoot certain species with a bow and arrow.

Sturgeon were once very abundant in the Bay and were reported in Potomac River fisheries until early in the twentieth century. They are all but extinct now in Virginia and Maryland waters. Both the shortnose sturgeon and the Atlantic sturgeon are listed as endangered on the Check List of the Biota of Lower Chesapeake Bay compiled by the Virginia Institute of Marine Science, at Gloucester Point.

Pound Nets

The use of pound nets changed the fisheries of Chesapeake Bay from a part-time, spring and fall avocation for farmers to a large and profitable industry. Not only were the catches increased greatly, but many commercially valuable species which had been unknown were caught in the pound nets.

The construction principle of a pound net is to hang a series of nets on poles to direct the fish into a large net bag which impounds the

Menhaden boats line the docks of Salisbury, Md., for winter layover and repairs. Maryland Department of Economic and Community Development

catch. Watermen usually fish the pounds once every 24 hours during slack water or the approximate turning of the tide. Preferably this is done between 4 and 9 a.m. Some pounds which have a variation called a pocket can be fished at any time of day.

Of interest to yachtsmen is the fact that each pound net must be marked by a white light at the head, at least 6 feet above normal high water and visible for one mile from all points of the compass and from the air, except in areas marked by buoys on the chart as fish trap areas.

The first pound net on Chesapeake Bay was set up by Capt. Henry Fitzgerald in 1858. It was badly constructed and unsuccessful, and so was soon dismantled.

The next pound nets on the Bay were built about 1870 by George Snediker and Charles Doughty of Fairhaven, N.J., a few miles above the mouth of the James River. They fished there for shad and alewives for about three years.

In 1875, Snediker constructed a pound net in Mobjack Bay which was so successful that the jealous local fishermen soon told him to take his nets and leave town. When he ignored the request, the local men sawed off the stakes holding the net at the water level, put the net on shore and threatened to destroy it if it was put out again. Snediker subsequently went to the Eastern Shore, became the partner of a popular fisherman there, and was thus able to avoid hostile feelings when he set up his next pound net.

Before Snediker left Mobjack Bay, he sold the sawed-off stakes to a fisherman who used them as samples for setting up his own pound net. Twelve nets were being fished in Mobjack Bay within a year of Snediker's departure. By 1880, they were scattered throughout Virginia waters and totaled 162 nets. In 1971, 1,436 pound nets were being fished in Virginia.

———

The first menhaden fishing industry on Chesapeake Bay started in 1865, when David G. Floyd of Greenport, N.Y., installed oil works on a sailing vessel.

In 1867, the first fish factory was built on Cockrell's Creek, a tributary of the Great Wicomico. Reedville, Va., founded in 1875, became the location for a fish factory which replaced an earlier one that was destroyed. Reedville, at the time of World War I, was considered the richest town per capita in the United States because of the wealth brought in by the menhaden industry. In 1972, Reedville still ranked as a leading fishing port where landings of nearly a billion fish were recorded.

Menhaden, members of the herring family, are also known as pogy, alewife, bunker and mossbunker. Some early Indians called the fish munnawhateaug; some others called it poghaden. Both names meant fertilizer. Indians showed the colonists how to plant menhaden with corn, and thus was begun the multimillion-dollar menhaden fishing industry we have today.

Now menhaden are also used in the manufacture of soap, stains, varnish, linoleum, heat-resisting paints, waterproofing compounds, and feed for fowl and stock. A by-product of menhaden fisheries, pearl essence, is a silvery substance found in the fishes' skin. This pearly product is used in the manufacture of lipstick, nail polish, costume jewelry and ceramics.

Menhaden, which migrate into Chesapeake Bay from the ocean during July, August, and September, are caught commercially in Virginia but not in Maryland. That is because they are most easily captured by purse seine, and such nets are legal in Virginia, but illegal in Maryland.

The heaviest catch of menhaden ever taken in Chesapeake Bay was 366,387,000 pounds in 1920.

Menhaden support the largest fishery by volume and the eighth most profitable fishery in the United States, and the most profitable fishery in Virginia.

Preliminary research is being done at the Chesapeake Biological Laboratory at Solomons, to determine if a fish commonly caught in Chesapeake Bay, called a hogchoker, has commercial value. If it is determined that the hogchoker will have sufficient consumer acceptance, it will probably be marketed under its alternate and more appealing name. A hogchoker by any other name . . . is an American sole.

The ugliest fish in the Bay is the toadfish. It is reportedly good to eat, but not many people eat it because of its repulsive appearance.

Sharks frequently come up Chesapeake Bay, sometimes swimming as far as tidal fresh water following the schools of small fish they feed upon.

Probably the largest shark reported in the Bay was a female bull shark, which measured about eight and one-half feet in length and weighed more than 328 pounds. It was captured in a pound net near Galesville, Md., in 1959, as was another shark over seven feet long and weighing about 200 pounds. The larger one bit an oar in two before being captured.

Bull sharks are sometimes called cub sharks, and two of them were taken in the Patuxent River in 1957. This shark is not a man-eater, but scavenges on fish, crabs, and other marine creatures.

Sandbar or brown sharks have also been captured in Chesapeake Bay. Scientists believe that the Bay is a spawning ground for this species.

In 1974, an 8-foot, 3-inch shark was captured in a pound net near Rock Hall, Md.

———

The common eel is really a fish that spawns in the Sargasso Sea and migrates back to fresh or brackish waters.

People who don't care to eat eels as the Europeans do may use them for bait. Champion rockfish and cobia have been caught using eel as bait, and salted eel is a common crab bait.

In 1974, about 18 tons, or 25,000 eels, were being exported by jet across the Atlantic from the Northern Neck of Virginia, to satisfy the gourmet appetites of Europe and Asia.

Near Colonial Beach, Va., George Robberecht has established the first United States eel farm with rearing ponds for baby eels, and he also has eel packing facilities in Montross and Cape Charles.

Nearly half of the eels caught in the United States come from Virginia waters, according to the National Marine Fisheries Service.

Other Marine Life

Jellyfish are among the oldest inhabitants of the earth. Their ancestry can be traced back more than 500 million years. Stinging jellyfish were first recorded in the New World in 1688, by Rev. John Clayton, who observed them from a becalmed vessel off the Virginia Capes.

In 1750, the *Maryland Gazette* reported that an Annapolis laborer who fell overboard from a small boat into the Rappahannock River became entangled in many sea nettles and drowned.

By 1966, Congress was providing funds on a matching basis to five states and Puerto Rico for sea nettle research. Although more than one million dollars has been spent, no way has yet been found to rid the Bay of jellyfish.

Stinging jellyfish are commonly called sea nettles. Their sting is intended to paralyze animal matter so that it can be eaten. The sting comes from the injection of a pure protein substance, which is why the application of a common meat tenderizer may neutralize the sting.

Various agencies are attacking the problem of sea nettles by: testing their tolerance to chemical control agents; developing physical barriers to protect swimming beaches from them; analyzing the stinging cells that are found on the body and tentacles of sea nettles; studying the life cycle of sea nettles to try to find a weak link in the cycle which might be exploited, and trying to find natural predators that might reduce the jellyfish population in the Bay.

Nonstinging jellyfish live in the Bay too, and these are known as comb jellies, water lights or sea walnuts. They are phosphorescent when disturbed and provide a beautiful, luminous trail for your boat as it moves through the water at night.

Among the natural enemies of the jellyfish which have been found are the sea slug, the harvest fish, the clingfish, and some of the blenny. None eat enough to materially reduce the sea nettle population.

———

Sea anemones are rarer than sea nettles, but they also have stinging cells. They spend their lives attached to rocks, pilings, shells, and seaweed.

———

Corals are also found in lower Chesapeake Bay, but they are not reef-forming. Oyster harvesters sometimes find a purple whip coral attached to shells.

———

Barnacles begin life as immature larvae with one eye, three pairs of legs, and a single shell. They drift with the current and moult until they have two eyes, six pairs of legs, and two shells. At this stage, they attach themselves to something, lose shells, eyes, and swimming legs, and grow a new, cup-shaped shell. Then a barnacle takes life easy, using the remaining feathery feet to propel food into its mouth as it floats by.

The glue a barnacle uses to attach itself is so strong that scientists are studying its composition with the idea of using it commercially, particularly in dentistry.

To give you some idea of how pestiferous barnacles are to vessels, take note of the report that a coastwise freighter picked up a growth of barnacles which weighed 40 tons and decreased her speed from twelve to four knots.

Ships coming to Baltimore frequently used to anchor for a period in the creek just below Jones Falls where the fresh water would kill barnacles clinging to the hull.

Shipworm!

Shipworms are long, bivalve mollusks. A shipworm's shell is only about ½ inch long, but its body can grow up to 12 inches long. Shipworms are apt to infest any bare wood exposed to the warm salt water of Chesapeake Bay during the summer months. The shipworm destroys the wood by tunneling into it, to make a place for itself as it grows. It tunnels by digesting the wood with enzymes, the only device the toothless worm has for drilling into the wood.

The marine turtles known as the diamondback terrapin were so common they were an annoyance to Bay fishermen in the seventeenth century.

Slaveholders were forbidden by a 1797 Maryland law to feed terrapin to their slaves more than once a week, lest they feed them the cheap and plentiful terrapin every day. Nowadays the terrapin is extremely scarce and costly, and is classified as a gourmet delicacy.

The diamondback terrapin, famous for the delicious soup it makes, was practically exhausted in the Bay by 1920, but was making a comeback by 1950. It seldom exceeds eight inches in length on the lower shell and a weight of 15 pounds. A length of five inches on the lower shell is the legal limit for keepers.

By law you may own not more than three terrapins which are being kept as bona fide pets. Would you put your pet in a soup pot?

Porpoises are more properly called bottle-nosed dolphin. They grow to eight or ten feet in length.

Seeing dolphin play in the southern part of the Bay is a thrilling experience for most people. They move through the water in schools, often riding the bow wake of a boat.

An English traveler in 1736 was less than thrilled, however, when his punt was overturned by frolicking dolphin which swooped against the side of his boat, dumping his luggage overboard.

A dolphin was reported seen in the Sassafras and Susquehanna Rivers area, unusually far north in the Bay for dolphin. It was noted in the Dec. 10, 1974 *Notices to Mariners* as an obstruction.

Harbor seals are occasionally seen in the Chesapeake, although they are regarded as transients. The young seals are chiefly observed in winter and may be as much as four feet long.

In the Miocene Age, the Chesapeake Bay climate was favorable for breeding whales, and evidence of their presence is often discovered in the Calvert Cliffs fossils.

Whales were not common in the Bay by 1710, but a Virginia resident applied for and received a whaling license in that year.

In 1746, a live whale 54 feet long was sighted and killed in the James River.

In 1747, John Custis, whose home was on the lower Eastern Shore of Virginia, made 30 barrels of whale oil from a whale which washed ashore on his beach.

In 1791, 1,263 gallons of whale oil were produced in Virginia.

Whales are still occasional visitors in Chesapeake Bay although none make their home there. In 1974, two whales excited Bay inhabitants. One, a fin whale, 53 feet, 8 inches long, was hit by a boat near the Portsmouth Marine Terminal and perished from the encounter. Another, a female pygmy whale about eight feet long, was found dead near Mathews, Va.

––––––––

The Smithsonian Institution's Stranded Marine Mammal Salvage Program would like to be notified of all whales, dolphins, and seals stranded or beached in Chesapeake Bay.

The stranded marine mammals are a source of information concerning a species' distribution, food habits, rate and causes of natural mortality, breeding season, and pesticide content.

Bay Area Wildlife

Wildfowl were once so plentiful on Chesapeake Bay that Capt. John Smith and two companions claimed to have brought down 148 ducks with three shots in the early 1600's.

Two other early Bay travelers wrote that the water was so black with ducks it sounded like thunder when they flew up. A colonist claimed he saw a square mile of ducks in flight.

––––––––

In November 1973, Canada geese and swans were at peak or near-peak levels in survey history in Maryland, making something of a comeback. Canada geese were estimated at 604,700, 139,000 over the previous high number, and 50,100 swans, compared with 16,700 in November 1972, were spending the 1973-1974 winter on the Maryland portion of the Bay, according to an aerial survey.

One reason for the increasing numbers of geese wintering on the Eastern Shore has been the introduction of the mechanical corn picker, resulting in greater food supplies left in the fields for the geese. The goose population in the Blackwater National Wildlife Refuge near Cambridge rose from a maximum of five thousand in 1942 to 100 thousand in the 1970's.

The goose population on the Bay is at its peak in November. The birds migrate from Canada when decreasing amounts of daylight, combined with weather conditions and other variables, tell them it is time. They fly in a V-formation to give each goose except the leader favorable air currents in which to fly. Older geese take turns leading. The normal migration altitude is only 3,000 feet, but geese have been seen flying as high as 29,000 feet. They feed on shoots and roots of aquatic plants in the marshes or on grain and greens in the fields. They are signaled to migrate north again by a reverse of the conditions which told them to come south, and most are gone from the Bay by mid-March.

A pair of geese usually mate for life. Five to eight eggs in a nest require 28 days to hatch.

———

Whistling swans winter in Maryland, Virginia and the Carolinas. To facilitate studying their habits, many have been banded, and a few have been fitted with small radio transmitters.

From reports on where these identifiable, banded swans have been sighted, scientists study their population structure, migratory pathways, family and group relationships, distribution, and longevity.

Great interest in studying whistling swans' migratory habits followed the crash of a Viscount airliner which collided with a flock of migrating swans in 1962, on Maryland's Eastern Shore.

To support or learn more about swan research, write to Swan Research Program, Johns Hopkins University, 615 North Wolfe Street, Baltimore, Md. 21205.

———

Mute swans are the largest waterfowl found in Chesapeake Bay, and they can be recognized by a black knob or shield over their orange bills. The mute swans may grow to a weight of 31 pounds and a wingspan of eight feet.

The original birds were imported from Europe to decorate estates along the Miles River. Some escaped on an extremely high tide in March 1962, and they have multiplied in the wild state.

Because they do not migrate, they eat and destroy large quantities of aquatic vegetation year-around. As their numbers increase, they are beginning to be considered a menace by some yachtsmen, fishermen and farmers.

———

An osprey is a large, fish-eating hawk. Its conspicuously crooked wings may have a spread of four and one half to six feet. They migrate from the Bay in September or early October to Brazil or Colombia, following the major river systems. They stay in South America until they are two or three years old, then return to the Bay in March to nest.

Ospreys make their nests of twigs and branches, but have also been known to include such odd items as old fishnets, rope, boards, large fish vertebrae, old cloth, an entire potato sack, cornstalks, vines, bark,

Varied contents of an Osprey nest

feathers, cork blocks from life preservers, a mop, and a broken canoe paddle.

Because of the destruction of some of their natural nesting habitat, ospreys frequently nest on man-made structures, where they are easily observed by yachtsmen and fishermen.

A recent survey showed that 31 percent of the Bay osprey nests were in trees, 29 percent on duck blinds, 22 percent on aids to navigation and 18 percent on other man-made structures.

Nearly one-half the ospreys reaching flying age in eastern Virginia were produced on aid to navigation structures in 1974, and there were 284 nests on aids to navigation throughout the Bay. The Coast Guard, which maintains these aids, does not remove the nests until they have been abandoned.

———

Though sea gulls are plentiful on Chesapeake Bay, young gulls are rarely seen because they breed on the ocean side of the Eastern Shore of Virginia and do not fly until they are fully feathered.

———

There are numerous deer in the wooded areas around the Bay. The Indians used to hunt them in the fall by setting fire to the woods to drive the animals into the water. Then they would spear or shoot the swimming deer with their bows and arrows.

———

One of the three wild herds of Sika deer in the United States is on James Island at the mouth of the Little Choptank River. The herd originates from four does and two bucks released there by Clement Henry of Cambridge, in 1918.

The Sika deer is really a miniature elk, native to Japan, which weighs only 40 to 60 pounds when full grown.

———

Wolves were considered a menace in the 1600's in the Bay Country. In Talbot County, 100 pounds of tobacco was offered for each wolf's head. Fifteen were redeemed in 1668, 14 in 1669, and 20 in 1672. In the early 1700's, a bounty was also paid for crows' and squirrels' heads.

———

The Delmarva Peninsula fox squirrel once roamed all over the Eastern Shore and north into Pennsylvania and New Jersey. It is protected against hunters, but faces extinction because its natural wooded habitat is disappearing due to forest fires, lumbering, and land clearing. The largest numbers of these big, gray squirrels may be found in the wildlife refuges, such as Blackwater and Eastern Neck, on the Eastern Shore.

———

Copperheads are the only poisonous snakes found in the Bay area. Spring and fall are its most active periods, and it hibernates in winter.

The snake can be recognized by its copper-red head, dark brown hourglass markings along its body, and pale belly with brown spots. Copperheads are not found in the water.

Fossils

The Calvert Cliffs are the best place in the entire United States to find certain types of fossils. The cliffs extend along the Western Shore of Chesapeake Bay for 35 miles, from Herring Bay to Drum Point. At their height of more than 100 feet, they are the highest land on the Western Shore of Chesapeake Bay.

The cliffs were formed during the Miocene Age, 14 to 20 million years ago. At that time, the climate was tropical in the Bay area, and porpoises, sharks, and whales shared the water with crocodiles, giant barnacles, coral, and other tropical fish and shellfish.

Fossils

Shells and bones which fell to the bottom as the creatures died were buried in the silt to become the fossils found in the cliffs and, to a lesser extent, in other areas around the Bay.

Miocene Age fossils commonly found are shark's teeth, coral, various seashells, whale bones, and crocodile plates. Teeth from a rare, ancient, seven-foot elephant have also been found.

In late 1968, a 20-million-year-old whale skull was found measuring five feet in length. Scientists speculate the whale must have been at least 100 feet long. In 1929, a seven-foot-long whale skull was found near Governor's Run, just north of Cove Point.

The very first fossil from North America described in Europe was the graceful Ecphora quadricostata, a spiral shell found on the Calvert Cliffs. After the unique find was taken across the Atlantic, the English author, Martin Lister, described and illustrated the shell in 1685. Now the same kind of shell may occasionally be found by lucky searchers in shallow water at the base of the cliffs. Scientists caution fossil seekers to stay off the cliffs themselves and to limit their hunting to the shallows along the Bay shore.

———

Other places to find fossils from the Miocene Age are along the banks of the Patuxent and St. Marys Rivers in Calvert and St. Marys Counties, along the Sassafras and Chester Rivers in Kent and Cecil Counties, and in the excavated banks of the Chesapeake and Delaware Canal. In Virginia, Westmoreland County's Nomini Cliffs along the Potomac contain remnants of past geologic ages. Located south of Colonial Beach, these fossil-bearing cliffs are situated near Westmoreland State Park, George Washington's birthplace and Stratford Hall, ancestral home of the Lees.

V. BOATS AND THE BAY

Built and Sailed on the Bay

No one knows exactly how the Indians came to Chesapeake Bay. We do know, however, that the earliest colonists made the trip from Europe in boats. The 104 Jamestown colonists came in the *Susan Constant*—79 feet, the *Godspeed*—50 feet, and the *Discovery*—39 feet. The first Maryland colonists came on the *Ark* and the *Dove*.

Boats were the most important means of transportation for the colonists. Realizing their importance, it took exactly one day for the Jamestown settlers to build a boat for themselves in the New World. According to George Percy, who was there, they began either to build or assemble a small boat on April 27, 1607, the day after they landed in the New World, and they launched it on April 28.

———

The dugout log canoe is the oldest indigenous Bay boat. The Indians had not yet learned the art of sailing and propelled their canoes with poles before the colonists came. The colonists bartered for some of the boats, copied and improved the design, and added sails.

The first sailing log canoes were made of only one, hollowed-out log. Later the canoes were made of three or five or more logs.

Although built to be used as fast cargo vessels, and for commercial fishing and oyster tonging, the log canoes were too unstable for these purposes.

Captain Bob Lambdin built 68 log canoes on Maryland's Eastern Shore between 1865 and 1894, probably more than anyone else. He once built a 25-foot, three-log canoe in just 20 days. That included choosing the trees and felling them. He is credited with installing the first centerboard in a log canoe.

Lambdin built a log canoe he called the *Chesapeake* and took her to the Chicago World's Fair in 1893. The canoe beat all challengers racing on Lake Michigan.

Organized log canoe races were first held in St. Michaels in 1840, with about 30 starters. A trophy or cash prize was awarded to the winner of these early races. A ham skin to grease the bottom of the boat and make it go faster was presented to the last-place boat.

At a good race these days, only about 15 log canoes assemble, and many of these have been rescued from conversions to powerboats. But at one time 175 log canoes were built annually and, in 1880, log canoes on the Bay numbered 6,300.

Two new log canoes under construction in the St. Michaels area in 1974 were expected to join the racing fleet when completed.

On Chesapeake Bay a brogan is not a shoe but a variation of a log canoe. Brogans, mostly later nineteenth century craft, were built like log canoes, but were usually bigger and had a different interior layout. The only one still under sail is thought to be the *Mustang*, berthed at Annapolis, where she is available for charter.

The *Mustang*, shown tied up in Annapolis Harbor, is thought to be the last sailing brogan remaining on the Bay. Anne M. Hays

The bugeye, a refinement of the log canoe, was built for oyster dredging and carrying cargo. For these purposes, she needed a strong and efficient sail plan, low freeboard amidships, and the shallow draft made possible by a centerboard so she could get into shallow creeks.

The log bugeye first appeared right after the Civil War. The first frame bugeye was built in Solomons by James T. Marsh, in 1879. The last wooden bugeye was built and launched in 1918. The first ferrocement bugeye is the *Eileen C.*, 35 feet long, built and owned by Jim Chamblee. Chamblee, a Savage, Md., boatyard owner and author of a technical book on ferrocement boat construction, launched his unusual craft in April 1973.

The Maryland law limiting the use of power for oyster dredging has perpetuated the use of skipjacks and bugeyes as commercial oystering boats.

Skipjacks tied up at Deal Island. Anne M. Hays

Why is a bugeye called a bugeye? Several theories have been advanced to explain such an unusual term for a boat. Some authorities attribute it to the Scottish word, bucklar, a type of boat. Or it may come from buckie, another Scottish word which means oystershell. One source says the hawse-holes look like bug's eyes, hence the name.

The skipjack on the right, tied up at Deal Island, is the *Robert L. Webster*, the largest skipjack ever built. Anne M. Hays

One of the oddest named bugeyes was *Brown Smith Jones*, the one-time flagship of the Maryland State Navy for enforcing oyster laws. The vessel, built in 1894, was named for three men, Maryland's governor, the comptroller, and the treasurer. Her dinghy was called *Tom, Dick and Harry*. *Brown Smith Jones* was commissioned as the U.S.S. *Dorchester* in the United States Navy during World War I.

The skipjack, a flat-bottomed, cross-planked, sailing boat with one fixed, raked mast, is an enlarged version of the bateaux that were built by colonists in the 1600's for crabbing, fishing, hunting, and oystering.

The skipjack is well suited to oyster dredging and is easier and cheaper to build than the log canoes, bugeyes and brogans which preceded it.

The last working skipjack to be built was the *Herman M. Krentz*, in Harryhogan, Va., in 1955. The 45-footer was named for her builder.

The largest skipjack is the *Robert L. Webster*, 60 feet long. She was built near Deal Island in 1915.

The *Florence Louise*, at 58 feet overall, is probably the second largest skipjack. She was built at Crisfield in 1924.

The 45-foot skipjack, *Minnie V.*, built in Wenona in 1906, is owned by the city of Baltimore and displayed in the Inner Harbor next to the *Constellation*.

The first boatyard in Maryland was in William Claiborne's settlement on Kent Island. A pinnace, the *Long Tayle*, said to be the first boat with sails and made of native wood to ply the Chesapeake's waters, was built there. The *Long Tayle* could accommodate 20 men. She took her name from the long wake the vessel trailed behind it.

Historians of early Bay life frequently mention a vessel called a shallop.

A shallop was a light, open boat, about 20 feet long, with one sail. It could also be rowed. It usually carried a crew of four or five men and cargo. At least three shallops were built at the Kent Island shipyard for William Claiborne, before 1637. They were called the *Star*, the *Firefly* and the *Cocatrice*.

The *Cocatrice* fought against Lord Baltimore's pinnaces, the *St. Margaret* and the *St. Helena*, in the first battle fought on water in Maryland.

In the early seventeenth century, colonists built only small coasting vessels because English and Dutch merchantmen carried all goods back and forth across the Atlantic.

Some commonly built boats in the Bay boatyards were: a sloop—a swift sailing boat, fore-and-aft-rigged with one mast which carried passengers and cargo; a barge—a bulky, square-ended freight boat which could be powered by either sail or oars, usually built of a native pine called deal; a wherry—a long boat powered by oars, used to carry planters and their families to church and on visits; and a mud scow—a flat-bottomed, square-ended boat for hauling nets or tobacco hogsheads.

In the latter part of the seventeenth century, European ships were scarce because of wars on the continent. So Bay builders began to build oceangoing ships with slimmer, lower hulls and higher masts than the old designs, and triangular sails.

A schooner is a sailing boat with two or more masts, all of which are fore-and-aft rigged, the mainmast being abaft of and taller than the foremast.

The first schooners were being built on Chesapeake Bay by 1730. They were fast, and so were used as privateers during the Revolution. Afterward they were used as pilot boats, sailing packets (a packet can be any kind of boat which travels a scheduled route), and freight carriers.

The only seven-masted schooner ever built, the *Thomas W. Lawson*, sailed on Chesapeake Bay. A picture of her under repair at the Newport News Shipbuilding and Drydock Company in 1906 also shows three-, four-, five-, and six-masted schooners being repaired there.

The last commercial sailing schooner on the Bay was the *Anna and Helen*, which sank in Crisfield Harbor in 1958.

The centerboard was introduced on Chesapeake Bay around 1815 and was first used on small schooners.

Baltimore Clipper was the name given to a type of ship built in the late 1700's and early 1800's which had the general characteristics of a schooner rig; long, light, extremely raking masts; low freeboard; and slack bilges. The design may have evolved from French luggers, which came over during the Revolution, or from a Swedish fishing boat, of a type built by Swedish immigrants around Baltimore.

The Baltimore Clipper was popular with privateers, slavers, smugglers, and pirates, who all needed fast boats about the time of the Revolution and the War of 1812. The end of the slave trade, peace with England, and a more lawful society caused these fast boats to go out of favor due to their limited cargo capacity. They disappeared around 1860.

Authorities say the name clipper probably came from the verb "to clip," meaning "to fly rapidly."

The *Ann McKim*, 143 feet long, with a 31-foot beam, was a ship-rigged Baltimore Clipper, a three skysail-yarder with royal studding sails. Built in Baltimore in 1832, she was the forerunner of the extreme clipper ships which were developed for the North Atlantic trade. She was sailed until 1847.

The *Rainbow*, built in 1843 by the *Ann McKim's* owners, copied many features of the *Ann McKim* and was the first extreme clipper ship.

The clipper ship's main advantage over the Baltimore Clipper was its increased carrying capacity.

———

The pungy evolved from the Virginia pilot-boat schooner and was in use by 1847. The pungy had a keel, deep draft aft, raking sternpost, flush deck, and two tall, schooner-rigged, raking masts with a main-topmast.

Pungys were used for oyster dredging and for carrying freight. Due to the deep draft of their keel, they were not able to get into shallow creeks, and they went out of style. The last one was built in the 1880's.

The last pungy sailed was *Wave*, built in 1862 and based on the Chester River until 1939. She was converted to a yacht and abandoned after going to the Great Lakes in the 1950's.

The *Amanda F. Lewis* was the last pungy to be actively sailed commercially. She carried freight on the Bay until 1939, then was converted to power to carry bananas from Haiti to Florida.

———

Rams were first built in 1889. The *J. Dallas Marvil*, the first ram, was also the smallest. She was only 112.8 feet long. Her 23.8-foot beam was just small enough to squeeze through the Chesapeake and Delaware Canal locks, which were 24 feet wide at that time. She cost $7,500 to build.

A ram can be described as a barge with sails. Rams were the largest commercial sailing design developed on Chesapeake Bay and usually carried lumber from the Carolinas. The ram had a bluff bow, high sides, a flat bottom, a centerboard and a three-masted, bald-headed rig. (Bald-headed means no topmasts.) Most of the rams were built on the Nanticoke River.

The rams *Levin J. Marvel*, *Edwin and Maud*, *Grace G. Bennett*, and *Mabel and Ruth* were converted to cruise ships which ran for a few years after World War II. Only the *Edwin and Maud*, renamed *Victory Chimes*, still sails as a cruise ship, out of Rockland, Maine.

———

A sloop is a single-masted, fore-and-aft rigged sailing boat with a single headsail set from the forestay.

Round-bottomed, gaff-rigged sloops were once commonly used for oystering on the Bay. The *J.T. Leonard*, a 55-footer built in 1882 on Taylors Island, is the last example of this type of boat. She is moored at the Chesapeake Bay Maritime Museum, in St. Michaels.

The *Elsie* was the last scow sloop (square-ended) to be sailed on the Bay. Because of the scow sloop's very shallow draft, they were commonly used in the northern Bay's shallow water. *Elsie* was abandoned about 1940.

———

A story about an old boat frequently ends with a line something like this: Went aground in a storm and sank with all hands. Variations on the theme are: burned at anchor; scuttled; rammed and sunk; converted to power; used for target practice, or rotting in a creek. A few examples follow.

On Aug. 12, 1724, several ships were wrecked on the James River in a hurricane.

The English merchantman *Rogers*, Capt. Wignell, from Liverpool to the colonies, was wrecked on the Middle Ground between the Virginia Capes in 1766. The crew was saved.

The *Peggy Stewart*, here shown in a model, was burned off Annapolis because she carried tea as part of her cargo, in 1774. Maryland Department of Economic and Community Development

The Scottish merchantman, *Earl of Chatham*, Capt. Wolsey, was sailing from Dublin to Maryland when she was lost near Cambridge in 1769.

The *Peggy Stewart* was a merchant ship owned principally by Anthony Stewart of Annapolis and named after his wife. After England imposed a tax on tea, Stewart tried to import some tea on the ship, and even agreed to pay the tax. This so incensed a local mob that they insisted Stewart set her ablaze, and she burned and sank off Windmill Point in Annapolis, Oct. 19, 1774.

The spot where she burned, then called Windmill Point because a large windmill stood there, has been filled and is now a part of the level space between Bancroft Hall of the Naval Academy and Annapolis Harbor.

The English ship *Totness*, Capt. Waring, was burned by Indians and totally destroyed near St. Mary's City, in 1775. No lives were lost.

In 1781, the British scuttled three American ships in the northern part of Chesapeake Bay.

At least six British warships and several smaller vessels were sunk during the British siege of Yorktown, in October 1781. Two of these wrecks were later found in 40 feet of water by fishermen who snagged their nets on them. The Mariners Museum of Newport News carried out salvage operations on them during the summers of 1934 and 1935. Cannon, cannonballs, swords, axes, tools, pieces of rigging, a brass ship's bell, and other items which are now on exhibit in the museum, were brought up.

Army divers claimed to have located 11 more wrecks in 1954.

September and October of 1785 were months of severe storms. Several large ships were sunk or destroyed. One particular gale at Portsmouth, Va., carried several large ships some distance into the woods.

The American merchantman *Betsey*, Capt. Tredwell, was loaded and preparing to sail for Liverpool when she accidentally burned at anchor at Norfolk and sank, in 1807.

The Canadian brig, *Hannah*, was wrecked at the mouth of the Potomac, in 1817.

———

The famous Civil War battle between the *Monitor* and the *Merrimack* took place in Hampton Roads, March 9, 1862. The battle, fought for four hours to a draw, was the first between ironclad vessels.

The *Merrimack* was destroyed by the Confederates shortly after the battle to keep her from falling into the hands of the advancing Union troops. The *Monitor* swamped, turned turtle, and sank off Cape Hatteras in a gale, Dec. 31, 1862. The wreckage was found but not recovered by a Duke University researcher, John Newton, in 1974.

———

Sometimes ships which are no longer useful for their original purpose can be used some other way. The U.S.S. *Valcour*, anchored at Point Patience on the Patuxent River on March 20, 1973. Three hundred and ten feet long, 41 feet wide, and displacing about 2,400 tons, she was built for a seaplane tender and launched June 5, 1943, but not commissioned until July 5, 1946.

After many adventurous cruises she will now serve as a test ship for studying the effects of electromagnetic pulses on her electronic equipment at the Naval Ordnance Laboratories at Point Patience.

The *Hannibal*, a freighter, ran aground west of Smith Island in 1944. The remains of the ship were used for target practice by surface vessels.

Steamboats

Because of the sheltered water, the big cities at the heads of navigation on the Western Shore, and the need for quick and reliable transport for farm and seafood products and for people, steamboats flourished on Chesapeake Bay from the beginning of the 1800's until the mid-1900's.

___

The very first steamboat on Chesapeake Bay waters was run experimentally by James Rumsey, on December 3 and 11, 1787, on the Potomac River. Rumsey's steamboat was driven by a power pump. The design was patented in 1791, but never became popular.

___

The first steamboat to run commercially on Chesapeake Bay was the *Chesapeake*, built at Flanigan's Wharf, in Baltimore. The *Chesapeake* was 130 feet long, with a 20-foot beam. Her paddle wheel was ten feet in diameter and five feet wide. She also had a mast with a spar and sail to be raised when the wind was fair.

Her maiden voyage was from Baltimore to Frenchtown on the Elk River, June 21, 1813, with Capt. Edward Trippe, one of her owners, in command. On this trip and the return, she traveled 140 miles in 24 hours. Passengers paid $1.25, meals included. On a trip from Baltimore to Annapolis later that same month, the fare was $1.00 each way.

Navigation methods were simple. There were no bells to signal the engine room. A pilot stood at the bow, called out the course to a man amidships, who relayed it to the helmsman. The captain gave his command either by word of mouth or by stamping his heels on the deck above the engine. According to one account, the boat had been running six months before the engineer accidentally discovered that he could reverse the engine and back her.

___

The *Philadelphia* was the second steamboat built in Baltimore, and the *Virginia* was the third.

The *Virginia* was fueled by 20 to 25 pitch pine logs every 15 minutes, or 2,000 to 2,400 logs for the 24-hour trip from Baltimore to Norfolk, making 6.4 knots under engine.

___

The first steamboat built in Norfolk was named the *Norfolk*. She was built in 1817. She made the trip to Baltimore in 20 hours.

The *Eagle*, 110 feet long, was the first steamboat to steam the length of the Chesapeake, on June 25, 1815.

The *Eagle* was only 20 feet wide and could set a sail in case of engine trouble.

Her boiler exploded April 24, 1824, killing one passenger, who was the Bay's first steamboat fatality.

Some of the well-known steamship companies on the Bay were: the Baltimore and Philadelphia Steamboat Co.; the Tolchester Co.; the Weems Line; the Maryland Steamboat Co.; the Eastern Shore Steamboat Co.; the Chester River Steamboat Co.; the Wheeler Line; the Choptank Steamboat Co.; the Wilson Line; and The Old Bay Line.

The Old Bay Line operated steamboats on the Bay for almost 125 years, having started operations in 1840 and ceased in 1962. At that time, she was the oldest steamboat line in the country.

On the early steamboats, the large passenger saloons were surrounded by a double tier of bunks. Thus, with tables in the middle, the room could be used both for eating and sleeping. The women had a separate sleeping cabin, but joined the men for meals.

Steamboats were often noted for the delicious meals served, although one disgruntled Frenchman wrote that they were totally without sauces and frills. And so they may have been, as the vegetables were cooked in steam drawn from the ship's boiler, and the meat was turned on a spit powered by the main paddle shaft.

The United States Coast Guard once stopped an Old Bay Liner by firing a shot at her, in March of 1929. The Coast Guard searched her and found what they were looking for—a car full of illegal whiskey.

The steamboat *St. Nicholas* was the first Union vessel to be captured by the Confederates, on June 28, 1861. Under Confederate command she captured the *Monticello*, the *Mary Pierce*, and the *Margaret*.

Richard Thomas, of St. Marys County, captured the *St. Nicholas* after boarding her disguised as a Frenchwoman, Madame Zarvona. He brought with him two trunks filled with arms. He and several fellow passengers took over the ship after it left Point Lookout.

Until 1959 when they were sold for scrap, two side-wheel steamers were used as icebreakers out of Baltimore, primarily to break a path between the Patapsco and Elk Rivers. The steamers had individually powered paddle wheels, could turn in their own length, and cut a path 65 feet wide.

The two steamers, the *F.C. Latrobe*, built in 1879, and the *Annapolis*, built in 1889, were the last side-wheel vessels to operate in the Chesapeake and the southernmost icebreakers in the United States.

Two 110-foot Coast Guard tugs based in Baltimore and one 180-foot Coast Guard buoy tender based in Norfolk now break the ice when necessary. A commercial tug, the *Carolyn*, especially outfitted for ice-breaking, can also be called upon by the Port of Baltimore if ice conditions become severe.

Because most boats are more powerful now than previously, fewer boats get stuck in the ice. Powerful tugs pushing barges are in themselves excellent icebreakers.

———

The *St. Mary's* burned after grounding on Holland Point Bar, in the Patuxent River, on Dec. 5, 1907. Afterward those aboard claimed they had seen the ship's mascot, a cat, jump ashore at the previous landing and disappear.

———

The steamboat *Express* broke up and sank in a hurricane on Oct. 22, 1878. She had departed from Baltimore and was to travel up the Potomac River, with her crew of 22 and nine passengers. Only eight persons were rescued.

The wife of Capt. Randolph Jones was one of the passengers. About the time the *Express* was to stop at Cross Manor, where the Joneses lived, Capt. Jones is supposed to have heard a knock. He looked out the window and thought he saw his wife beckon him to the front door. All of this happened about the same time the *Express* went down, and Mrs. Jones drowned.

———

Steamboats which survived catastrophic destruction, but which became outdated or proved uneconomical to run, were often converted to floating restaurants, motels, or clubs, or were used as bulkheads, or freighters, or barges, or as barracks or supply ships during World War II.

The *Chauncey M. Depew* was built for the Maine Central Railroad in 1913. In 1924, she became a day cruiser for the Hudson River Day Line. During World War II she was a troop transport. After World War II she cruised the Bay, sometimes on the Baltimore to Tolchester Beach run. In 1950, she went to Bermuda to work in Hamilton Harbor. She was brought back to Chesapeake Bay in 1970 and was grounded in Jones' Bass Hole in North East, Md., in 1971. She was sold again and raised in 1973 and redecorated for restaurant duty.

The old *Tolchester* was renamed the *Freestone* and became a club moored to the end of a pier at Freestone Point, Va., in 1957. The alcoholic beverages sold aboard and the slot machines she carried were illegal in Virginia, but legal in Maryland, which owns the Potomac River up to the low water mark on the Virginia shore. This attempt to circumvent the restrictions of the Virginia law was scuttled when a law was passed in 1958 stipulating that such a club would not be legal unless it could be reached by foot from the Maryland shore.

Eight Bay steamboats requisitioned by the United States government sailed together from St. John's, Newfoundland, for England, in 1942. Three of the steamers were sunk by submarines, but the other five made port and served during World War II in various capacities in Europe.

One Bay steamboat, the *President Warfield*, became the *Exodus* in 1947. She was used to illegally transport Jews from France to Palestine. A total of 4,554 persons made the trip, although she had been rated for a capacity of 540 during her days on the Bay. She eventually caught fire at her mooring in Haifa Harbor, Aug. 26, 1952. Her remains were sold for scrap.

Ferries and the Bridges that Replaced Them

Travelers have depended on ferries to transport them with their vehicles and their goods across the Bay and its tributaries since 1638. In that year, the first ferries were established in both Virginia and Maryland and they were a necessity until the twentieth century when bridges became common.

Maryland's first ferry, which was specifically used to carry the burgesses to St. Mary's City, is said to have been the first public utility in the New World.

Adam Thoroughgood's small brick house in present-day Virginia Beach now stands amid modern suburban homes and is open to the public. Thoroughgood started one of the first ferries in the colonies. His craft was a skiff rowed by slaves between Norfolk and Portsmouth.

The fare on a Sassafras River ferry established in 1650 between Ordinary Point and the present site of Kentmore Park was an English shilling, or about 15 cents.

In 1811, when Richard Jones was granted a license to run a public ferry from Kent Island to Annapolis, ferry charges were still in shillings and pence. In 1812, charges began to be made in dollars and cents.

In 1705, 20 ferries crossed the James River, 20 served the York River and its tributaries, eight were on the Rappahannock, one on the Potomac and two crossed the Bay from Northampton to Yorktown and to Hampton. By 1748, the number of ferries in Virginia had doubled.

The ferry across the York River from Yorktown to present-day

Gloucester Point was operated continuously from 1705 until a bridge was built there in 1952. Two and a half centuries must be somewhat of a record!

In 1757, one of the five ferries in Norfolk was a free ferry supported by county funds to provide passage for poor people on their way to market.

———

Many people remember riding on the ferries between Annapolis and Matapeake on Kent Island. This ferry was the main route between the Western Shore and the Eastern Shore and the ocean beaches for 22 years.

The service was begun July 5, 1930, as an additional route for the company which already ran ferries from Annapolis to Claiborne (Claiborne is located on Eastern Bay, northwest of St. Michaels). The private company running the ferries was taken over in 1942 by the state which ran it as the Chesapeake Bay Ferry System.

Before the ferries were replaced by the William Preston Lane Jr. Memorial Bridge in 1952, the traffic lines which backed up past Stevensville on Sunday nights to wait for ferries to the Western Shore were legendary. Waiting people played cards or catch to pass the time and bought sandwiches and cold drinks from vendors who strolled up and down the lines.

———

As early as 1705, a ferry was crossing from the eastern shore of Virginia to Yorktown, Norfolk and Hampton. That route eventually became the Little Creek Ferry System, the busiest ferry service in the world. Seven ships were making the 85-minute crossing several times each day before the Chesapeake Bay Bridge Tunnel was opened in April 1964. The flagship of the Little Creek Ferry System, the S.S. *Pocahontas*, was 367 feet long, could carry 1,200 passengers and 120 vehicles. She made the last ferry crossing on April 15, 1964.

———

Other Bay area ferries still running can be counted on the fingers of one hand. In Virginia, the Sunny Bank ferry takes Route 644 across the Little Wicomico River near Smith Point.

The Jamestown-Scotland ferry links the two banks of the James River on Virginia Route 31.

Another Virginia ferry is the Merrypoint ferry carrying Secondary 604 traffic over the Corrotoman River in Lancaster County.

Maryland's remaining ferries are on the Eastern Shore. Upper Ferry crosses the Wicomico River south of Salisbury at the crossing between Eden, Md., and Quantico Road. The White Haven ferry crosses from White Haven to Mt. Vernon in Somerset County and is used by commuters to Crisfield and Princess Anne.

The last ferry in Dorchester County ran across the Transquaking
River. The ferry was a scow whose length was half the width of the
river and the whole vessel was pulled across the water on a rope.

This ferry crosses the Wicomico River on a cable. Maryland Department of Economic and Community Development

The best known remaining Chesapeake ferry connects Oxford and
Bellevue. Recent research indicates that the ferry was first established
by Richard Toylston in November 1683. He was appointed by the Tal-

bot County courts to "Keepe a ferry for horses and Men from His Plantacon over Tred Haven Creeke to the towne of Oxford and Back againe or on board any Shippe Nigh there Riding." For this he was paid 2,500 pounds of tobacco annually.

The ferry had several other operators until 1699, when Judith Bennett and her succession of three husbands, Richard Bennett, John Valliant and Edward Elliott, ran the ferry for 38 years. Judith Bennett was the first of several women ferry keepers on the Tred Avon.

After the Revolutionary War began and the tobacco trade with England died, the ferry ceased to run. It began service again in 1836, and may have operated continuously since then.

Capt. Benson is the best known modern keeper of the Tred Avon ferry. He operated it almost single-handedly from Feb. 21, 1938 to July 1, 1974. His longest vacation during that time came when the ferry was frozen in from Jan. 5 to March 16, 1940.

Though the ferry was first a rowed barge (for horses and vehicles) and a sailboat (for foot passengers), it had become a diesel-powered boat accommodating both vehicles and passengers by the time of Capt. Benson's retirement.

Capt. Gilbert Clark followed Capt. Benson as owner and operator of the Oxford-Bellevue ferry. Under his management a new ferryboat which can carry six cars, *The Southside*, took over the route. The smaller *Tred Avon* used by Capt. Benson was sold as a pleasure boat to a new owner on the South River.

––––––

When the first bridge across the Bay to the eastern shores of Maryland and Virginia was opened in 1952 near Annapolis, it was "the longest all-steel bridge over salt water in the world." Traveling at 40 mph, a vehicle takes six and one-half minutes to cross the bridge.

Within 20 years, traffic had increased enough to make a second span necessary. It was completed in 1973, 450 feet to the north of the first bridge. A comparison of their statistics follows:

	New	Old
Length	3.98 miles	4.35 miles
Width	38 feet, curb to curb (3-lane)	28 feet, curb to curb (2-lane)
Cost	$118,000,000	$41,000,000
Main Channel Span—Length	1,600 feet	1,600 feet
—Height	186.5 feet above mean high water	186.5 feet above mean high water
Eastern Channel Span—Length	780 feet	780 feet
—Height	63 feet above mean high water	63 feet above mean high water

Both bridges curve so they will cross the main ship channel at right angles.

Both spans are now known as the William Preston Lane, Jr. Memorial Bridge. Lane was governor of Maryland when the original span was completed.

———

Spanning the mouth of Chesapeake Bay, the Chesapeake Bay Bridge-Tunnel was designated "The Outstanding Engineering Achievement— 1965," by the American Society of Civil Engineers and called "One of the Seven Wonders of the Modern World."

The Bridge-Tunnel spans 17.6 miles, including two mile-long tunnels 98 feet under the ship channels, one high bridge, four 8-acre islands and 12 miles of low-level trestle only 30 feet above the water. It takes 23 minutes to drive across and saves approximately 95 miles and one and one-half hours of driving time between Norfolk and New York City.

A fishing pier and restaurant are located on the southernmost island. Travelers may stop there for meals, snacks and free fishing.

The Bridge-Tunnel took three and one-half years to build and cost about $200,000,000.

———

A concrete and steel bridge crossing a channel dividing upper and lower Hoopers Island opened in Sept. of 1980. At the dedication, as reported by the Baltimore *Sun*, those attending bowed their heads and the invocation was delivered as follows: "Father, today we are gathered here to dedicate a bridge that is a monument to man's stupidity, a monument to man's waste, a monument to governmental interference and inefficiency."

The bridge replaced an old, wooden plank structure, has a vertical clearance of 27 feet and can be seen over the Dorchester marshes for two miles. From an original estimate of $500,000, the cost had risen to $3.5 million by the time it was completed.

The man who delivered the invocation said his friends told him after-ward what he said "was right," but his timing "was not right."

———

The Thomas Johnson Memorial Bridge across the Patuxent River near Solomons links Calvert and St. Mary's counties. The 1.37-mile span cost $34 million to build, and was dedicated on Dec. 17, 1977. It is named for the first governor of Maryland who was born in Calvert County.

Before the bridge was built, Capt. Leon Langley ferried employees of the Patuxent River Naval Air Station across the river in his boat, the *Miss Solomons*, twice a day, from 1941 to 1977, without a single accident.

———

The Francis Scott Key Bridge arches over the Patapsco River from Hawkins Point to Sollers Point near Fort Carroll in Baltimore Harbor. Its four lanes rise 185 feet above the water, cover a distance of 1.6 miles. Including 8.7 miles of approach roads and structures, the structure cost $140 million. The bridge, named for the author of "The Star Spangled Banner," opened in March, 1977.

VI. COMMERCE ON THE CHESAPEAKE

Natural Resources and Trade

The founders of Virginia hoped the colonists would find gold and silver to send home to make them rich. When these treasures were not discovered, the Virginia colonists and the Maryland colonists who soon followed were encouraged to send home raw materials such as lumber, furs, fish, and even sassafras roots. The colonists in return needed finished goods from England. And so the tradition of trade and business was established on the Bay, based on the natural resources of the New World.

Glass was the first manufactured commodity in the New World. It was made at Jamestown, in 1608. A reproduction of the glasshouse has been built to demonstrate to visitors how the glass was made then.

The first English-built road in America connected Jamestown to Glasshouse Point, where the glass factory stood. The road, built in 1608, was one mile long. Later the road was extended to Governor Berkeley's plantation, about four miles from Jamestown.

For a time, the colonists hoped to get rich by exporting furs. For example, William Claiborne shipped furs to England worth around 5,000 pounds sterling in the 1630's. In 1652, Col. Edmund Scarburgh sold 72 moose skins to an English merchant for 10 shillings each. In the early 1700's, beaver, otter, raccoon, buck, and doe skins were exported to England from Virginia. But duties imposed on furs, to provide funds for the College of William and Mary, were so high that trade became unprofitable. The fur trade never prospered again, even when duties were finally lowered, although muskrats are still trapped for their pelts today in limited quantities along the Eastern Shore.

The colonists needed salt to preserve fish and other foods necessary to keep from starving as well as for export. Since salt was very expensive to import, they tried to make it themselves. Sir Thomas Dale, governor of Virginia, sent a group of men to the Eastern Shore in 1614 for this purpose. They made salt there for a few years by digging ponds and letting the water evaporate from them, leaving a salt residue. In 1630, Governor John Harvey of Virginia designed and set up a factory on the Eastern Shore to make salt. The venture was tried there because the peninsula was narrow enough to enable the men to use salty water from the ocean side in the boilers and ship the salt to Jamestown from the Bay side.

A bushel of salt weighing 70 pounds could be obtained by boiling down 250 to 300 gallons of seawater.

When Col. Edmund Scarburgh improved the apparatus for making salt, the Virginia Assembly promised him two shillings and sixpence per bushel, plus 10,000 pounds of tobacco, if he could make 800 pounds of salt for the colony in 1660.

Old pond used by early Virginians to make salt on the Eastern Shore. Eastern Shore Chamber of Commerce

Later, a few colonists made their own salt. Judge John Beale Bordley made salt from the water of the Wye River during the Revolutionary War to prove it was possible to get along without trading with England.

By the 1620's, tobacco had become the leading product of the Chesapeake colonies. It was easy to grow, and smoking the weed had become fashionable, even though King James considered it dangerous and unhealthful.

By 1700, Maryland and Virginia were said to be worth one million pounds sterling a year to England, based on tobacco, shipping used, and English-manufactured goods consumed by the colonists.

By 1775, the colonies exported 100,000,000 pounds of tobacco to England, worth around $4,000,000. Tobacco constituted about three-fourths of all commodities exported from the colonies of Maryland and Virginia at that time.

Newport News is still the world's largest tobacco port.

Tobacco caused the oldest recorded organized protest against taxation without representation in America. This was the Northampton Protest, drawn up by the Eastern Shore Virginians who had no voice in the Jamestown Assembly which had imposed the tax on tobacco.

Tobacco Barn

Tobacco eventually began to wear out the soil, so farmers planted grain instead. Chestertown, Md., became a grain exporting center for the surrounding farmland. From 1770 to 1775, Chestertown, on the Chester River, exported 130,000 bushels of wheat, 5,000 barrels of flour, and 50,000 bushels of corn a year. Georgetown, Md., now a leading yachting center on the Sassafras River, exported 50,000 bushels of wheat, 3,000 barrels of flour, and 10,000 bushels of corn. Worton, Fairlee, and Gray's Inn Creeks were smaller grain exporting centers at that time on the Eastern Shore.

Over half the wheat raised in North America was produced in Maryland and Virginia by 1830. Richmond and Baltimore competed for the title of major flour milling center of the country. In 1834, the world's largest flour mills were said to be the Gallego Mills, in Richmond.

————

Fertilizer was needed to replenish the soils depleted by excessive tobacco culture. When someone discovered that seabird guano from the coast of Peru could be shipped profitably to the Chesapeake Bay area, visions of empire quickly took shape.

One entrepreneur, Peruvian Frederick Bareda, had plans to ship guano for fertilizer to Solomons, which had a deep natural harbor. He built himself an elaborate house and planned to build a railroad from Baltimore to Drum Point. The Wall Street Panic of 1873 caused that venture to be abandoned.

In 1856 Capt. Edward Cooper, in the bark *Abbotsford*, found guano on islands near Haiti and this was imported to Baltimore.

Founding of the chemical fertilizer industry in the United States is claimed by Baltimore. In 1849, Phillip and William Chappell were granted the first patent for making compound fertilizers there. Fertilizer is still one of Baltimore's main exports.

————

Silk culture was tried in 1623 in Virginia, as an attempt to increase exports. The colonial Assembly directed that mulberry trees be planted and even passed an act in 1656 which mentioned silk as a profitable commodity. If a tobacco planter failed to plant at least ten mulberry trees for every 100 acres of land he owned, he was subject to a fine of 10 pounds of tobacco.

This venture failed because the problem of getting silkworms to grow in the Virginia climate was overlooked by the advocates of silk culture, as was the lack of skilled labor needed to convert the cocoons into thread. Mulberry trees, however, still flourish in Tidewater Virginia.

Silk culture was tried in the 1830's in Talbot County, on Maryland's Eastern Shore. The scheme was promoted by a Pennsylvanian, Samuel Whitmarsh, who made a fortune selling farmers slips of the white mulberry tree to grow, first to produce more trees to sell and then to feed silkworms. By 1839, an Easton newspaper estimated that 100,000 white mulberry trees had been planted within a one-mile radius of Easton. Shortly thereafter someone discovered that growing silkworms and converting their cocoons to silk required unavailable skilled labor, and so the scheme failed, just as it had in colonial Virginia.

————

In 1847, Charles Carroll, namesake and grandson of a signer of the Declaration of Independence, heard there was a market for black cat fur pelts in China. So he set out to raise black cats for their fur. He bought a supply of black tomcats and had an agent advertise for 1,000 female black cats at 25 cents each. He put all these cats on Poplar

Island, which he owned, thinking the surrounding water would yield a supply of fish to feed the cats and provide a natural barrier to their escape. It might have worked, except for the unusually cold winter and the resulting ice bridge to shore which provided the cats with a means of escape.

Escape from the Black Cats Fur Farm

The first ironworks in the colonies was set up near Richmond, Va., at Falling Creek, in 1619. It was destroyed in the 1622 Indian massacre. By 1730, Virginia had five iron furnaces. At one time there were seven furnaces on a 10-mile stretch of the Potomac River below Alexandria. The Accokeek Furnace on Virginia's Northern Neck became one of the largest furnaces in the colonies. By 1750, it yielded about one-sixth of all iron produced in both Maryland and Virginia.

An act of the Maryland Assembly in 1719 offered 100 acres of land as an incentive to establish an iron furnace. The Principio Furnace in Cecil County was established in the 1720's and produced half the iron exported by Maryland at that time.

By 1762, Maryland listed eight iron furnaces and ten forges.

In 1970, the industry had grown and evolved so that the world's largest steel mill was located in Baltimore.

Coal was needed to fuel the iron furnaces. North America's first coal mine was located along the James River, in Chesterfield County, Va. From 1735 it produced most of the nation's coal supply for almost a century.

Until recent years, boats were the primary freight carriers to small Bayside towns. Within the last 20 years, the number of these local freight vessels has dwindled rapidly. In 1958, 44 motor freight craft were moving from town to town around the Bay and its tributaries, most of them carrying grain. Now only about six vessels haul grain, mostly from the Western Shore of Virginia to elevators in Norfolk and Baltimore.

One remaining craft is the 146-foot motor vessel *The Virginian*, captained by William E. Bowen. From July to Christmas, Capt. Bowen hauls grain. The rest of the year he and other captains haul slag for road building to the Eastern Shore from Sparrows Point, Bethlehem Steel's Baltimore plant.

Bay Ports

One hundred and ten million tons of waterborne commerce moved on Chesapeake Bay in 1970, and that amount has increased since. The portion of it destined for Baltimore has made that port the single most important economic resource in Maryland.

The port of Baltimore was founded in 1706, preceding the founding of the city by 23 years.

The port now has 45 miles of waterfront. Its tidal range of 13 inches is the lowest for any United States seaport. An estimated 4,500 ships from 47 nations use the port annually. One hundred and eight steamship lines have 272 monthly sailings from it.

In 1974, Baltimore expected to handle a record 41 million tons of import-export freight. The more than two million tons of container freight handled in 1973 ranked Baltimore as the second largest among all United States East Coast ports in that category.

The most important export commodities are coal, corn, soybeans, soybean meal, iron and steel products, automobiles, and trucks. The most important commodities imported are iron ore, coke, gypsum, sugar, and petroleum.

Baltimore has long been a center of the shipbuilding industry on the Bay. The first frigate of the Continental Navy was outfitted there, as were the first two Navy cruisers. In 1849, Baltimore builders produced the only oceangoing steamer built outside New York City. In 1890, the first steam tanker built in America, *The Maverick*, was launched by a Baltimore firm. The first Liberty Ship, *The Patrick Henry*, was launched by Bethlehem-Fairfield Shipyard, Inc., of Baltimore, on Sept. 27, 1941.

Frozen food is loaded onto a ship bound for England in Cambridge, Maryland's port. Maryland Department of Economic and Community Development

Two other ports in Maryland also serve oceangoing vessels. Cambridge, on the Choptank River, is built on land purchased from the Choptank Indians for 42 matchcoats (an old type of cloak). Named for Cambridge, England, it was first a port of entry in 1683. The port now covers 13 acres. The channel is 26 feet deep. The chief product handled there is frozen fish.

Another port is at Piney Point, on the lower Potomac River, where Steuart Petroleum handles bulk shipments of petroleum products.

Another port for oceangoing vessels in Maryland is planned for completion in 1977. This will be at Cove Point, near Solomons, where imported liquefied natural gas will be handled. This facility is now under construction.

———

Virginia ports are administered by the Virginia Port Authority. Portsmouth, Newport News, and Norfolk, all in the Hampton Roads area, share preeminence as Virginia's leading port. Other ports in the state are Hopewell and Richmond on the James River, and Alexandria on the Potomac River.

According to the Port Authority, 90 steamship lines sail from Virginia ports, with a ship leaving a state port every 15 hours bound for Europe. Mediterranean-destined vessels depart every 16 hours. If you want to go to the Pacific, there is a ship departing once a day. Ships bound for Africa and the Middle East are less frequent, with sailings every 45 hours.

Seventy motor carriers and five major rail systems converge on the Hampton Roads complex to support this extensive trade.

The Hampton Roads area is considered one of the world's greatest natural harbors and is formed by the confluence of the James, Nansemond, and Elizabeth Rivers. It is 45 feet deep, ice-free at all times, well protected from winds, and has very little fog.

The Hampton Roads complex is an important shipbuilding center. The world's largest privately owned shipyard, the Newport News Shipbuilding and Drydock Co., is located there. It has built such vessels as the *Enterprise*, of World War II fame, and the *United States*, the world's largest passenger ship.

———

Norfolk has been a leading port and center of commerce on Chesapeake Bay since the 1700's. Her early importance stemmed from the presence nearby of agricultural crops, lumber, and naval stores. Shipbuilding facilities were good, and trade with the West Indies was brisk. Many products were sent for export to Norfolk from North Carolina because that colony lacked deepwater ports.

Norfolk has continued to grow in volume of trade. Its 1973 trade of $4.1 billion was 25 percent over the 1972 level, and its significance as a container port has increased rapidly.

Norfolk is the leading coal exporting center of the world.

Wind, Water and Tide Mills

Three different styles of windmills were constructed around the Bay in the seventeenth, eighteenth and nineteenth centuries. One was a Dutch type, called a smock mill because its octagonal wooden structure with a movable cap resembled a figure dressed in a smock. The second type was called a tower mill and was constructed of stones or bricks with a movable top. The third type, or post mill, had a tower that turned on a pivotal post. When it swung, the wings then were set at the proper angle to the wind.

————

Windmills were popular laborsaving devices with early settlers in the Bay area. In 1621, Gov. Yeardley built a windmill in Virginia, the first such building to be constructed in North America. Prior to 1634, William Claiborne's men built two large windmills for grinding grain and to supply power for other tasks on Kent Island.

Windmill

On March 1, 1641, the first windmill to be built on the Eastern Shore of Virginia was contracted for by Obediance Robins and John Wilkins. Anthony Lenny, the millwright, was paid 220 pounds sterling and 20 barrels of corn for his labor and the materials needed to build the mill. Robins and Wilkins furnished the ironwork and shingles.

By 1649, four windmills, five water mills and a number of horse- and hand-driven mills had been built in the colony of Virginia. In 1776, a windmill on Point Comfort was used as a landmark in Anthony Smith's sailing directions for entering the James River.

Windmills were more popular in Dorchester County, Maryland, than elsewhere around the Bay because water mills did not work very well where the land is so flat. Known locations of windmills in Dorchester County are: near Church Creek; at Tobaccostick; on Taylors Island (3); in Lakes District (2); on the Blackwater River; on the Bennett farm near Cambridge; and on the Radcliffe farm near Lloyds.

This latter windmill was destroyed in 1888 by a tornado which blew its 16-foot-wide base completely out of sight.

In 1973, the windmill was reconstructed in honor of ex-Senator George M. Radcliffe by his son and others who formed a foundation to do the work.

A miller was frequently a retired sailor who used his knowledge of handling ship's sails to handle the sails of the windmill. If the wind got too strong, a windmill's sails, like a ship's sails, had to be reefed so the mill would not grind too fast.

———

Colonists also used the tides to power mills on Chesapeake tributaries. The wooden mill wheel powering the grinding stones was geared to turn one way with the incoming tide and to reverse with the ebb tide.

A tide mill was built in colonial times near Bushwood Wharf at the mouth of the Wicomico River, and another is known to have stood near the Nomini Cliffs along the Potomac.

The only Chesapeake tide mill still standing is on the East River which flows into Mobjack Bay. According to records, the tide mill there ground grain for General Washington's army during the siege of Yorktown in 1781.

———

Mills whose wheels were powered by water flowing in only one direction were the most commonly built on Chesapeake tributaries.

Because it was often necessary to dam a stream to raise the water level enough to turn a mill wheel, and because one man often owned land on only one side of a stream, a 1705 law gave a potential mill-builder a way to acquire some land on the stream's other bank.

The law said that if the mill was considered necessary, the prospective mill-builder could buy one acre across the stream from his own land. The price was determined by mutual agreement or sometimes by arbitrators. When the mill stopped operating, the land reverted to the original owner. There was one stipulation: the mill had to be started within one year of the land purchase and be completed within three years.

An early colonial law stated that each customer was to have his grain ground in turn and no one could take another's place in line.

A town called Head of Chester (so named because it was located at the head of navigation on the Chester River) once was a milling center. Within a radius of three miles, at least six water-powered mills were in simultaneous operation in the 1800's.

The town later was renamed Millington, not because of the mills, but in honor of a prominent family. No members of the family were millers by trade.

Canals

In 1661, Augustine Herrman made the first recorded proposal to build a canal across the 14-mile-wide peninsula separating the Delaware River and Chesapeake Bay. Through the years many other men suggested that such a canal be built, including Benjamin Franklin in 1788.

When the canal finally was built, it shortened the water route from Baltimore to Philadelphia by 316 miles and to New York by 179 miles.

Several routes were proposed for the canal before it was started. One route would have followed the Chester River and another the Sassafras River to shorten the distance to be dug. In 1764, a survey team measured the Delmarva Peninsula for the purpose of laying out a canal route, but no action was taken.

When excavation for the canal actually began, the route followed the Elk River and its tributary, Back Creek, across the land to Delaware City.

In 1799, the legislatures of Maryland, Pennsylvania and Delaware passed acts incorporating the Chesapeake and Delaware Canal Co. Maryland bought $50,000 worth of stock, Pennsylvania $100,000, Delaware $25,000 and the U.S. Government $450,000. The remaining $1,625,000 worth of stock was sold to the general public. Digging began in 1804, but was discontinued in 1806 for lack of funds. Construction resumed in 1823 and the canal was completed in 1829.

Because it was too expensive for a private company to maintain and improve, the federal government bought the canal in 1919 for $2,500,000. It is now maintained by the U.S. Corps of Engineers.

The Chesapeake and Delaware Canal was opened Oct. 17, 1829. At that time it was 13 miles long with a waterline width of 66 feet, a bottom width of 36 feet and a depth of ten feet.

The canal had four locks. Two of them were located at Chesapeake City, the western end of the canal. One was at St. George's, Delaware, and one was at Delaware City, the eastern end of the canal. The lock at Delaware City is the only one still in existence and it is no longer part of the actual canal. The locks were originally 96 feet long and 22 feet wide. In 1854, they were enlarged to 220 feet in length and 24 feet in width. After several more deepening and widening projects, the locks were eliminated in 1927.

The canal presently has a waterline width of 600 feet, a bottom width of 450 feet, with a depth of 35 feet.

An early advertisement for the canal read in part, "The rates of Toll have been fixed so low as to make this the cheapest as well as the most expeditious and safe channel of communication between the waters of the Chesapeake and Delaware.

"Horses for towing vessels may be hired at reasonable prices at each end of the Canal."

Later boats were pulled through the canal by shallow-draft tugs.

Long, slender and tall ships were built especially to carry more passengers and freight through the narrow C and D Canal. The *Lord Baltimore*, whose record run of 24.56 mph made her the fastest steamboat on the Bay before she was scrapped in 1933, was 200 feet long and only 23 feet, 6 inches wide.

The *Ericsson*, built to similar dimensions and unstable due to the great height of her decks and her narrow beam, was caught in a gale near Wilmington, Del., turned over on her side, and sank in shallow water, drowning one passenger.

An undocumented story tells of one of these steamers going to the aid of a yacht in distress in Chesapeake Bay. The steamer passengers rushed to one side to watch the rescue, causing their own ship to list alarmingly. Thereafter, the story goes, men were stationed in the ship's hold to roll full casks of water from one side to another to balance the ship.

The Chesapeake and Delaware Canal saved Washington, D.C., for the Union when southern troops threatened to attack in the early days of the Civil War. Northern troops rushing to the city's defense found the railroad bridges across the Susquehanna River had been burned by southern sympathizers. Ships commandeered in Philadelphia harbor were able to make the trip through the new canal, pick up the stranded soldiers at Perryville on the north side of the Susquehanna River and ferry them to Annapolis. From there it was a short trip to Washington and the city was held for the Union.

The first bridges over the Chesapeake and Delaware Canal were lift bridges. Frequently the spans and piers were rammed and knocked down by ships. Now all four highway bridges are high enough for ships to pass beneath.

The freighter S.S. *Waukegan* rammed the bridge at St. George's in 1939. It was rebuilt as a high level bridge in 1942.

The motorship *Franz Klassen* rammed the lift bridge at Chesapeake City in 1942. A ferry replaced it until the new high-level bridge was built in 1949.

The lift bridge at Summit, Delaware, was replaced by a high-level bridge in 1960 and was the last one to be modernized.

Because the original railroad bridge bisected the worst bend in the canal, the present railroad bridge was built over dry land. In 1966, the channel was diverted under it, straightening the troublesome bend. The bridge has a horizontal clearance of 548 feet, making it one of the longest of its type ever built.

When the canal was cut, fossil formations were exposed dating from as long ago as 135 million years. The government has set aside some areas where amateurs may collect fossils which are chiefly mollusks. Specific information on collecting areas is available from the C and D Canal Museum in Chesapeake City.

The fossils are primarily of the steinkern type. That is, they are the internal mold left when the shell was filled with mud which later hardened and the shell itself dissolved.

Fish and reptile bones, including vertebrae and teeth, have also been found in the canal banks and bottom spoil.

Bridge over the C & D canal

In 1783, a company was chartered to build a canal above Havre de Grace on the Susquehanna River. In 1800, $150,000 had been spent, and the canal was not yet completed. In 1817, the project was abandoned. Sometime during those years, the *Baltimore Evening Post* commented, "More money than water is being poured into the Port Deposit Canal."

In 1839, the canal was finally opened and it became one of the busiest canals in the United States within two years. About one-third of the traffic coming from the west went to Philadelphia via the C and D Canal; the remaining two-thirds went to Baltimore. In its best year, 1864, the canal earned $300,000.

In 1870, the Susquehanna and Tidewater Canal was leased for 999 years by the Reading Railroad to carry coal. The railroad made no improvements and the canal was ruined by floodwaters in 1894 and abandoned after 54 years of use. Some ruins of the canal and a lock may be seen about one-fifth of a mile north of Shenk's Ferry.

The first commercial canal in the United States opened in 1790. It
ran from Richmond to Westham, paralleling the James River for seven
miles. George Washington was one of the prominent Virginians who
invested in the James River Company which built the canal.

The canal was extended to Lynchburg in 1840, a distance of 156
miles. In 1851, it was extended to Buchanan. The canal was destroyed
by floods and the ravages of the Civil War.

Lights

The first Chesapeake Bay lighthouses were built on points of land
because no one knew how to construct a lighthouse that would stand
up on the Bay's soft, mucky bottom. Between 1791 and 1910, more
than 100 lighthouses were erected at 74 locations on Chesapeake Bay.

Bodkin Light, built in 1822 and the first to be constructed in Maryland, stood on land at the mouth of the Patapsco River. Another beacon was built on Poole's Island in 1825. However, these were quite
unsatisfactory because a light on shore could not definitely mark how
far a shoal extended into the Bay.

Someone thought of marking the tip of a shoal with a lighted, anchored ship. The first lightship in the United States was anchored off

Lightship Chesapeake

Willoughby Spit on the south side of the entrance to Hampton Roads in 1820. But the water there was too rough for the small decked-over boat, so it was sent to Craney Island to mark the mouth of the Elizabeth River.

Four more lightships were placed on station the following year and by 1825 there were ten on Chesapeake Bay.

The lightship *Chesapeake*, relieved from her regular duties where she marked the mouth of Chesapeake Bay, now serves as a laboratory where Potomac River plant and fish life are studied. She is docked at a pier off East Potomac Park, in Washington, D.C., and is open to the public for free tours. Write Lightship Chesapeake, 1200 Ohio Drive, S.W., Washington, D.C. 20242 for details, or call 202-426-6897.

Other former lightships may be toured at the Chesapeake Bay Maritime Museum in St. Michaels, Md., and in both Hampton and Portsmouth, Va.

Lightships were not a trouble-free solution to the problem of marking dangerous waters. They were occasionally rammed and sometimes parted their anchor lines in bad weather.

In 1774, the state of Virginia assembled most of the materials necessary to build a lighthouse at Cape Henry, but discontinued work because of the Revolutionary War.

The newly created Federal Lighthouse Service took over the project in 1791, completing the Cape Henry Lighthouse and first lighting it in 1792. The octagonal sandstone structure, the first to be built by the new United States Government, still stands at Fort Story, Virginia Beach, but is no longer lit.

Close by the old lighthouse, a newer Cape Henry lighthouse stands. Built in 1881, its iron tower is 164 feet tall and its light flashing every 20 seconds can be seen for 19 miles. The great beacon is painted with vertical alternate black and white stripes which distinguish it from any other lighthouse and from its background, as well. The new Cape Henry light became the first radio-distance-finding station in the world in 1929.

The present Cape Charles Lighthouse is an iron tower built in 1895 on eastern Virginia's southernmost tip and marks the north cape entrance to Chesapeake Bay. Reaching 191 feet above the land, it is the tallest lighthouse in service in the United States. The light is untended, gives off 200,000 candlepower and is rated as visible for 20 miles. (Lights may be seen at greater distances than normal because of refraction of the light under certain circumstances, or may be obscured at the normal range due to fog, rain, snow or haze.)

The distinctive black and white stripes on the Cape Henry Lighthouse distinguish it
from any other lighthouse. Anne M. Hays

The Cove Point Lighthouse, a white stone tower on shore north of the Patuxent, was built in 1828. For many years the keepers there, in addition to tending the light, identified any ships moving up the Bay and reported their imminent arrival in Baltimore harbor.

Two Coast Guardsmen and their families are on duty at Cove Point Light and it has the distinction of being the last family light station on the Bay.

The light can be seen for 18 nautical miles on a clear night.

An Englishman, Alexander Mitchell, invented the screwpile method of lighthouse construction which worked well on Chesapeake Bay. As suggested by the name, the individual pilings were corkscrewed down into the soft bottom until they formed a stable base for construction of the lighthouse.

The first screw-pile lighthouse on the Bay was built on the Pungoteague River and survived only 459 days before succumbing to ice floes, making it the shortest-lived lighthouse on the Chesapeake.

Three more screw-pile lighthouses were built soon afterward: in 1855 in the lower James River at White Shoal, Point of Shoals and Deep Water Shoals.

The first lighthouse of this type built in Maryland was located at Sevenfoot Knoll at the mouth of the Patapsco River, in 1855. In 1971, the house was donated to the Mariners Museum by the Coast Guard and it was scheduled to be sent to its new location by barge.

Until builders learned to protect the legs of the lighthouses with piles of stone rip-rap, many of the structures shared the fate of the first one on the Pungoteague River and were carried away by the ice. On Feb. 10, 1881, the unprotected Sharp's Island Light was damaged and the next winter yet another screw-pile lighthouse on Solomons Lump, between Smith and South Marsh Islands, came down.

After World War II, the screw-pile lighthouses began to be phased out as manned structures and converted to automatic status. Authorities decided at first to leave the empty buildings intact for easy daytime identification of the lighthouses.

By 1958, however, many of the wooden buildings were dilapidated. A basic design was drawn up to remove the keeper's house and erect a steel tower on each base to elevate the light. Most of the screw-pile lighthouses have now been modified to this design.

Thomas Point Light, a hexagonal screw-pile lighthouse, is the only one of its kind still manned on the Chesapeake in 1975. Built in 1875, the light that has been tended for over a century is scheduled for automation in 1977.

MH

Thomas Point Light

A similar lighthouse which once stood in Hooper Strait is now preserved at the Chesapeake Bay Maritime Museum, in St. Michaels, Md.
Another hexagonal lighthouse, Drum Point Light, near Solomons at the
entrance to the Patuxent River, still stands, but is inoperative. A func-
tional light has been mounted nearby. The Drum Point building is now
the property of Calvert Marine Museum and is scheduled for relocation
to the museum grounds in Solomons.

The only remaining screw-pile lighthouse in Virginia is the one built at White Shoal in the James, in 1855. Privately owned, it does not function as an aid to navigation.

———

The caisson base lighthouse was an improvement over screw-pile construction. To build one, a cylinder was hauled to the chosen spot, driven into place and filled with concrete to serve as a base for a house and light.

Only 12 caisson base lighthouses were built on Chesapeake Bay and the last one to be erected in Maryland waters is the Baltimore Light, commissioned on Oct. 1, 1908.

Caisson lighthouses are all unmanned, having been gradually automated over the years. Smith Point Light, at the mouth of the Potomac, was the last lighthouse with keepers living on it. It was finally automated in 1971.

Many caisson lights may be seen easily from shore. From north to south, the lights are: Craighill Channel Forward Range, Baltimore, Sandy Point, Bloody Point, Sharps Island, Hooper Island, Point No Point, Solomons Lump, Smith Point, Wolf Trap, Thimble Shoal, and Middle Ground.

———

Several of the Chesapeake Bay lighthouses were raided and the lights destroyed by Confederate guerrillas during the Civil War. Among these were: the Cape Charles Lighthouse, raided in 1862 and relit in 1864; the New Point Comfort Lighthouse, attacked sometime during the war and not relit until 1865; the Cape Henry Lighthouse, lantern destroyed early in the war and replaced in 1863; and the St. Clements Island Lighthouse, raided in 1864 and relit only several days later.

The lightships on Smith Point and Wolf Trap Shoal were both raided in 1861. A new lightship was stationed at Smith Point in 1862.

———

What has happened when a light goes out? In one case, investigators found the keeper of the Holland Bar Light was dead, and had probably been murdered.

Nowadays most lights are unmanned, and their function is not interrupted by such human catastrophes. Everything is operated electrically and monitored by a photoelectric alarm system. Even burned-out light bulbs can be automatically replaced.

———

Many women served as lighthouse keepers. Frequently a woman inherited the job from her husband when he died.

The last woman lighthouse keeper in the United States was Mrs. Fannie Salter, who served from 1925 to 1947 as keeper of Turkey Point Light, near the head of Chesapeake Bay.

A lighthouse keeper on Chesapeake Bay received an annual wage of $640 in the 1890's.

———

The oldest lighthouse in continuous service in the United States was built in 1827 and stands on Concord Point, near Havre de Grace. Lighthouses may have stood in some locations longer, but the original structures are no longer in use.

———

On June 8, 1974, the 6-second flasher at the junction of Mill and St. John Creeks, tributaries of the Patuxent River, was observed to flash 557 consecutive times before settling down to its regular pattern.

BIBLIOGRAPHY

BIBLIOGRAPHY

Aymar, Brandt, *A Pictorial Treasury of the Marine Museums of the World.* (1967) Crown Publishers, Inc., New York, N.Y.

Barbour, Philip L., *The Three Worlds of Captain John Smith.* (1964) Houghton Mifflin Company, Boston, Mass.

Beitzell, Edwin W., *Life on the Potomac River.* (1968) E.W. Beitzell, Abell, Md.

Blair, Carvel Hall and Willits Dyer Ansel, *Chesapeake Bay: Notes and Sketches.* (1970) Tidewater Publishers, Cambridge, Md.

Blanchard, Fessenden S., and Stone, William T., *A Cruising Guide to the Chesapeake.* (1962) Dodd, Mead and Company, New York, N.Y.

Bodine, A. Aubrey, *Chesapeake Bay and Tidewater,* Bodine & Associates, Baltimore, Md.

Brewington, M.V., *Chesapeake Bay Log Canoes and Bugeyes.* (1963) Tidewater Publishers, Cambridge, Md.

——, *Chesapeake Bay: A Pictorial Maritime History.* (1956) Bonanza Books, New York, N.Y.

Brown, Alexander C., *Steam Packets on the Chesapeake.* (1961) Cornell Maritime Press, Cambridge, Md.

Bruce, Philip A., *Economic History of Virginia in the Seventeenth Century.* (1907) The Macmillan Company, New York, N.Y.

Burdett, Harold N., *Yesteryear in Annapolis.* (1974) Tidewater Publishers, Cambridge, Md.

Burgess, Robert H., *Chesapeake Circle.* (1965) Cornell Maritime Press, Cambridge, Md.

——, *This Was Chesapeake Bay.* (1963) Cornell Maritime Press, Cambridge, Md.

——, *Chesapeake Sailing Craft,* Part I. (1975) Tidewater Publishers, Cambridge, Md.

Burgess, Robert H., and H. Graham Wood, *Steamboats Out of Baltimore.* (1968) Tidewater Publishers, Cambridge, Md.

Chandler, J.A.C., and Thames, T.B., *Colonial Virginia.* (1907) Times-Dispatch Company, Richmond, Va.

Chapelle, Howard I., *The Baltimore Clipper.* (1965) Tradition Press, Hatboro, Pa.

DeAngelis, Richard M., and Hodge, William T., *Preliminary Climatic Data Report Hurricane Agnes.* (1972) Asheville, N.C.

deGast, Robert, *The Lighthouses of the Chesapeake.* (1973) Johns Hopkins University Press, Baltimore, Md.

Earle, Swepson, *The Chesapeake Bay Country.* (1938) Thomson-Ellis, Baltimore, Md.

Edmunds, Pocahontas Wight, *Tales of the Virginia Coast.* (1950) Dietz Press, Richmond, Va.

Footner, Hulbert, *Maryland Main and the Eastern Shore.* (1967) Tradition Press, Hatboro, Pa.

———, *Rivers of the Eastern Shore.* (1944) Tidewater Publishers, Cambridge, Md.

Forman, H. Chandlee, *Old Buildings, Gardens and Furniture in Tidewater Maryland.* (1967) Tidewater Publishers, Cambridge, Md.

Geddes, Jean, *Fairfax County Historical Highlights from 1607.* (1967) Derlinger's, Middleburg, Va.

Guide to Charles County, Maryland. (1974) Charles County Chamber of Commerce, La Plata, Md.

Gutheim, Frederick, *The Potomac.* (1949) Rinehart and Company, New York, N.Y.

A Hornbook of Virginia History. (1965) Virginia State Library, Richmond, Va.

Huelle, Walter E., *Footnotes to Dorchester History.* (1969) Tidewater Publishers, Cambridge, Md.

Jones, Elias, *New Revised History of Dorchester County Maryland.* (1966) Tidewater Publishers, Cambridge, Md.

Lang, Varley, *Follow the Water.* (1961) John F. Blair, Winston-Salem, N.C.

Maryland, A Guide to the Old Line State. (1940) Compiled by the Writers' Program of the Work Projects Administration in the State of Maryland, Oxford University Press, New York, N.Y.

Mason, Samuel Jr., *Historical Sketches of Harford County.* (1940) Published by author. Intelligencer Printing Company, Lancaster, Pa.

Middleton, Arthur Pierce, *Tobacco Coast, A Maritime History of Chesapeake Bay in the Colonial Era.* (1953) The Mariners Museum, Newport News, Va.

Preston, Dickson J., *Wye Oak: The History of a Great Tree.* (1972) Tidewater Publishers, Cambridge, Md.

Richardson, Hester D., *Sidelights on Maryland History.* (1967) Tidewater Publishers, Cambridge, Md.

Richardson, R.H., Edited by, *Chesapeake Bay Decoys: The Men Who Made and Used Them.* (1973) Tidewater Publishers, Cambridge, Md.

Semmes, Raphael, *Captains and Mariners of Early Maryland.* (1937) Johns Hopkins Press, Baltimore, Md.

Sherwood, Arthur W., *Understanding the Chesapeake.* (1973) Tidewater Publishers, Cambridge, Md.

Shosteck, Robert, *Weekender's Guide.* (1973) Potomac Books, Inc., Washington, D.C.

Stein, Carles F., *History of Calvert County.* (1960) Published by author in cooperation with Calvert County Historical Society, Schneidereith and Sons, Baltimore, Md.

Thomas, M.C., *Fossil Vertebrates, Beach and Bank Collecting.* (1968) Sunshine Press, Venice, Fl.

Tilp, Frederick, *Potomac River Weather Folklore.* (1970) Privately printed.

Titus, Charles W., and Thomas E. Jones, *The Old Line State: Her Heritage.* (1971) Tidewater Publishers, Cambridge, Md.

Virginia, A Guide to the Old Dominion. (1940) Compiled by the Writers' Program of the Work Projects Administration in the State of Virginia, Oxford University Press, New York, N.Y.

Virginia Department of Conservation and Development, *State Historical Markers of Virginia.* (1948) Virginia Division of Publicity and Advertising, Richmond, Va.

Wain, Sidney and Estell, *Waterway Guide.* Mid-Atlantic edition. (1974) Sidney J. Wain, Inc., Washington, D.C.

Wilstach, Paul, *Tidewater Maryland.* (1931 reprinted 1969) Tidewater Publishers, Cambridge, Md.

——, *Tidewater Virginia.* (1929) Tudor Press, Indianapolis, In.

Wise, Jennings Cropper, *Ye Kingdom of Accawmacke or the Eastern Shore of Virginia in the Seventeenth Century.* (1911) The Bell Book and Stationery Company, Richmond, Va.

INDEX

Cape Henry Memorial, 22
Carolyn, 109
Carroll, Anna Ella, 58
Carroll, Charles, 120
Carter, Robert (King), 39
Carter's Grove, 40
Carvel Hall, 64
Casemate Museum, 41
Caulk's Field, 64, 65
Cedar Point (Potomac), 69
Center for Environmental and Estuarine
    Studies, The, 17
Chamblee, Jim, 99
Chapel Point, 39
Chappell, Phillip, 118
Chappell, William, 118
Charles I, King, 25, 28
Charles II, King, 63
Charlestown, 45
Charlottesville, 21
Chasseur, 55
Chauncey M. Depew, 109
Cheriton Creek, 65
Cherrystone Inlet, 83
Chesapeake, 41, 42
Chesapeake (lightship), 38, 128, 129
Chesapeake (log canoe), 98
Chesapeake (steamboat), 107
Chesapeake Bay Bridge Tunnel, 43
Chesapeake Bay Center for Environ-
    mental Studies, The, 16
Chesapeake Bay Foundation, The, 17
Chesapeake Bay Institute, The, 16
Chesapeake Bay Maritime Museum, 35,
    36, 104, 129, 132
Chesapeake Bay Model, 17
Chesapeake Biological Laboratory, The,
    16
Chesapeake City, 34, 125, 126, 127
Chesapeake and Delaware Canal, 83, 97,
    104, 125, 126
Chesapeake and Delaware Canal Mu-
    seum, 34, 127
Chesapeake Research Consortium, 15
Chester River, 2, 25, 97, 104, 117, 125
Chestertown, 7, 8, 45, 47, 61, 64, 69, 71,
    117
Choptank River, 2, 3, 15, 17, 29, 30, 54,
    121
Christ Church, 39
Church Creek, 58, 124
City of Norfolk, 6
Claiborne, 111

Claiborne, William, 6, 41, 55, 58, 102,
    115, 123
Clams, 83-84
Clark, Capt. Gilbert, 113
Clayton, Rev. John, 89
Clinton, 39
Coan River, 39
Coan Wharf, 39
Coast Guard Museum, 42
Cocatrice, 102
Cockburn, Admiral, 62
Cocklescroft, 54
Cockrell's Creek, 87
Coleman Bridge, 83
Colonial Beach, 39, 44, 89, 97
Concord Point, 134
Constellation, 31, 102
Cooper, Capt. Edward, 118
Cornwallis, Lord, 67
Corrotoman River, 85, 111
Coursey, Col. Henry, 25
Cove Point, 96, 122
Cove Point Lighthouse, 131
Crabs, 79-83
Craighill Channel Entrance Lighthouse, 5
Craighill Channel Forward Range Light-
    house, 133
Craney Island, 129
Crisfield, 17, 26, 27, 46, 81, 102, 111
Crisfield Harbor, 103
Cross Manor, 109
Custis, Daniel Parke, 59
Custis, John I, 58
Custis, John II, 59
Custis, John IV, 59, 92
Custis, John V, 59

Dale, Sir Thomas, 23, 27, 115
Dale's Gift, 27
Davis, Jefferson, 41, 56
Deal Island, 46, 67, 100, 101, 102
Debedeavon, 51, 65
Debtors' Prison, 43
Decatur, Commodore Stephen, Jr., 37
Deep Water Shoals Lighthouse, 131
Delaware City, 125
Delaware, Lord, 23
Discovery, 98
Dixon, Jeremiah, 63
Dorchester, U.S.S., 101
Doughty, Charles, 87
Douglass, Frederick, 59
Dove, 7, 51, 58, 98